YOUR LAW, MY DELIGHT

YOUR LAW, MY DELIGHT

Daily Devotions Inspired by the Torah

BY

MARCI WALKER PURTELL

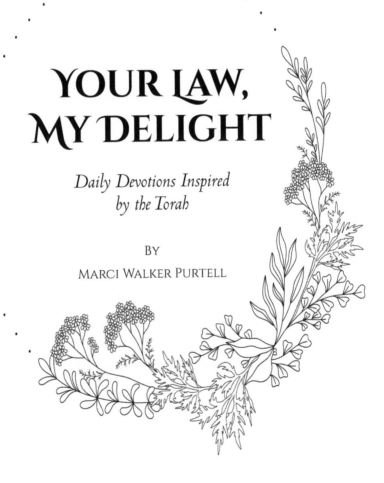

PALMETTO
PUBLISHING
Charleston, SC
www.PalmettoPublishing.com

Hardcover ISBN: 979-8-8229-4194-6

Paperback ISBN: 979-8-8229-4195-3

eBook ISBN: 979-8-8229-4196-0

Dedication

Jesus, thank you for loving me and giving Your life for me.
Vance, thank you for seeing the gift in me and choosing me.
Randal and Alathia, thank you for teaching me. I love you more.
Mom and Dad, thank you for giving me wings.
Pastor Olen and Syble, thank you for counseling, guiding, and
pastoring me.

Blessed is the man who...his delight is in the law of the Lord.
Psalms 1:1-2 (NKJV)

If your law had not been my delight, then I would have
perished in my time of trouble.
Psalms 119:92 (AMP)

CONTENTS

Very Good. 1

Thus Noah Did. 4

He Settled There 5

Dumb Fear 7

May I Refresh Your Heart 9

Graciously Remembered, Graciously Visited 12

Behold Him. 14

The Promise Keeper 16

He Sees. 19

Forgiveness and Reconciliation 24

Dream a Little Dream. 27

Favor 29

Hurry! Change Your Clothes!. 32

God Sent Me 34

Settled in the Best 36

My Shepherd 39

Encounter: A Holy Flame 41

Now Go!. 44

Just a Finger 46

For Their Sake 48

Two Pillars 51

Shabbat: A Holy Gift 53

Honor's Reward 55

The Only One 57

Dwelling Place 60

Sweet Aroma 62

Be the Buffalo. 64

Uniquely Radiant 67

Stirred Up 69

Qualified. 71

Seasoned with Salt 73

Always Burning. 76

Regard Him. 79

Make a Distinction 81

As I Am 84

Two Goats. 87

Offered Freely. 90

Feasts Forever. 93

A Purposeful Pause 96

A Peaceful Portion. 98

Professional Movers 100

A Child Tended Him .102

The Aaronic Benediction. 105

Leaders Sacrifice 108

You Will Return 110

It's Too Heavy. 112

Reading the Report 114

Posture of Defense. 117

A Gift to Me 119

Balaam's Donkey. 121

Beautiful, Blessed Israel. 124

Serah, Daughter of Asher, a Warrior 126

Rash Words, Serious Consequences 129

The Final Stand: A War for Worship 132

Regrets—My Idol Worship. 135

Cities of Refuge 138

Yet for All This... 140

The Good Life 142

Why Do You Love Me! 145

A Good Land 148

Clingy 151

Brighten Up. 154

For Dana. 156

The Best Neighbor. 160

Brought Out to Bring In 163

Secret Keeper 166

Choose Wisely 168

Moses—May His Memory Be a Blessing. 170

VERY GOOD

Then God saw everything that He had made, and indeed it was very good.
So the evening and the morning were the sixth day.

—Genesis 1:31 (NKJV)

My son, Randal, preached his first sermon when he was five to an audience of one—me. It was a tough parenting day, and I had lost my temper—again. I am ashamed to admit I did that often in those early days, and sadly, it wasn't uncommon for me to raise my voice. And as was my typical response after such an outburst, words of shame and self-loathing soon bubbled out of my mouth and would not stop.

As I was rehearsing what a terrible person and parent I was, Randal raised his little voice and uttered his first sermon: "No, Mom! You're not terrible! The Bible says God saw everything he made and said it was good. He made you. You are good!"

The fight drained right out of me. As I stood speechless before my son, unsure of the way forward, something a good friend had shared years before came to mind. When I asked her for parenting advice before Randal was born, she advised me to become skilled at repenting. She explained that I would mess up often and being quick to repent was crucial in those

1

moments. Her advice to me that day—to repent quickly—was all I could do. I repented to Randal, and his words were etched deep within me.

I remember the boy Randal once was and realize he is still tender, kind, helpful, funny, creative, and wise, albeit taller, older, and more mature.

I have heard many good sermons, and his first one ranks near the top. All that God made is good, or *tobe* in the Hebrew: good, beautiful, pleasing. He made all of creation, including you and me, and we are good, pleasing, and beautiful in His eyes. May that simple yet profound truth transform our hearts.

Self-Reflection: I will miss the mark in every relationship we have; therefore, repentance is a gift I will offer. May repentance, not remorse, define my relationships. As Poet Eliza Cook wrote in *Diamond Dust*, "Remorse is the poison of life, and repentance its cure."

Prayer: Father, thank You for Randal and for Your Word. Thank You for how You lovingly teach and guide me. You are good, and You keep doing good. Your leadership in my life is perfect, and You can be trusted. Amen.

Daily Reading: Genesis 1–3

THUS NOAH DID

Thus Noah did; according to all that God commanded him, so he did.

—Genesis 6:22 (NKJV)

And Noah did according to all that the Lord commanded him.

—Genesis 7:5 (NKJV)

God asked Noah to do something radical—build an ark in a place where rain did not exist. It wasn't just any ark—it was huge. Given that Noah's generation was corrupt, I can only imagine the ridicule Noah endured—yet Noah obeyed. And as a result of Noah's belief in and obedience to God, Noah was found righteous (Gen. 7:1).

Additionally, Noah's obedience to God profoundly impacted his family. The Bible teaches us that his sons saw what Noah was doing and they went with him. Considering that many Bible scholars estimate it took 120 years for Noah to build the Ark, I have to wonder if Noah's sons ever questioned his actions or if they trusted him immediately. During the time Noah built the Ark, I imagine Noah took time to explain everything God spoke to him and at some point along the way, each son chose to trust their dad because he was a man of integrity. His actions and words aligned with his faith; his sons saw that day after day, nail after nail, board after board. Noah's relentless belief in and obedience to God protected and provided for his family. As parents, it was essential for my husband and me to share our faith and struggles with our children so they could see our relationship with God lived out. God gave us a mandate before they were born—to raise children who passionately pursued God and worshipped Him alone which begins with their personal relationship with Him. Whether you are a parent, a leader, or a mentor, may we be inspired to follow Noah's example in teaching those who follow us what it means to hear and obey God's voice.

Self-Reflection: Whatever God is asking of us to do, it is not as radical as building an ark. May we, like Noah, be found obedient.

Prayer: Father—forgive me for not heeding Your voice at times and going my own way. Give me grace and courage to obey your voice in everything so I might be a testimony to those around us. You are good, and You can be trusted. Your leadership in my life is perfect. Amen.

Daily Reading: Genesis 4–7

HE SETTLED THERE

One day Terah took his son Abram, his daughter-in-law Sarai (his son Abram's wife), and his grandson Lot (his son Haran's child) and moved away from Ur of the Chaldeans. He was headed for the land of Canaan, but they stopped at Haran and settled there. Terah lived for 205 years and died while still in Haran.

—Genesis 11:31-32 (NLT)

I have always loved the story of Abraham because it is one I identify with—out of obedience to God, Abraham left his father's home for a land God promised (chapter 12).

But as I read this passage leading up to Abrahm's departure, I realized that his father, Terah, left his father's home first.

Terah lived in Ur with his family. He married and had children, and after one of his sons died, he left Ur for the land of Canaan—but he stopped and settled in Haran, where Terah eventually died.

As a parent and a leader, this is a passage that piques my curiosity. Why did Terah leave Ur? Did God direct him to? Was he fleeing the place that held memories of his third son? And why did he decide to settle in Haran when it was not his original destination—what changed?

Bible scholars estimate that Haran was a little over halfway to Canaan. Perhaps they stopped in Haran to rest and replenish their supplies. Terah was an artisan who made idols, and he was likely able to sell or trade his idols in Haran for much-needed supplies and food. Perhaps the journey to Canaan was hard and what he had intended to be a reprieve in Haran became "home" because it was easier than the journey. Whatever Terah's reasons were for leaving home and settling in Haran, we know that Terah never achieved what was once his heart's desire. He died in Haran, never making it to Canaan all because he chose to settle.

Self-Reflection: I wonder if there is an area of my life, or yours, where we are "settling" simply because it is more comfortable. What has God put in our hearts to do that remains unfinished? Fear and complacency are chains that have bound me in the past. Are they still?

Prayer: Father, search my heart. Show me if I am settling. Have You given me an assignment I am leaving untouched or unfinished? God, at the end of my life, I want my testimony to be that I poured out everything for You. Search me, speak to me, and lead me. Your leadership in my life is perfect, and You can be trusted. Help my unbelief. Amen.

Daily Reading: Genesis 8–11

DUMB FEAR

After these things the word of Adonai came to Abram in a vision saying,
"Do not fear, Abram. I am your shield, your very great reward."

—Genesis 15:1 (TLV)

Abraham is one of my favorite people in the Bible. I identify with him and can easily imagine what it must have been like to take his family, leave the only home he'd ever known, and start a journey with no clear destination. We have done that—following God through two states and thirteen moves during our marriage.

Then, after having the courage to leave home, Abraham told a *big* lie about Sarai being his sister because he was afraid. Pharaoh took her into his home, and God intervened by sending a plague to Pharaoh and his household. Pharaoh immediately kicked Sarai out of his home and confronted Abraham with his lie—a lie spoken solely out of fear. Fear led Abraham to make a dumb decision. I get it! I have done some dumb things, too, simply because I was afraid!

Further on the journey, Abraham inherited the land of Canaan and separated from Lot, his nephew, later rescuing him with 318 mighty men Abraham trained for war. After rescuing Lot,

Abraham refused a reward to maintain his integrity. Then, after all these things—stepping out in faith, being afraid, lying, and attacking a people to rescue his family—God appeared in a vision and spoke these words to Abraham: "Do not fear." While the phrase "do not fear" or "do not be afraid" appears in various places throughout scripture, if my research is correct, this is the first time God spoke it.

In the Hebrew text, the word for "shield" indicates a covering like the scales of a crocodile (H4043) and the word for "reward" means restitution, wages, or provision (H7939). Simply put, God is saying, "Do not worry—stop being so terrified. I am your covering, I have your back, and I will provide all you need where I lead you."

Self-Reflection: Whatever we face, may we remember He is for us, His way and plans are perfect, He is good, His leadership is perfect, and He can be trusted. Is God asking you to do something crazy—like move to a different state? Do not fear. Did you sin because you were afraid and got caught? Do not fear. Repent.

Prayer: Adonai, forgive me for the many times I have disobeyed you. Forgive me for lying and deceiving others out of fear. I am afraid. Deliver me from a spirit of fear and help me to trust You. Amen.

Daily Reading: Genesis 12–15

MAY I REFRESH
YOUR HEART

Then the Lord appeared to him by the terebinth trees of Mamre, as he
was sitting in the tent door in the heat of the day. So he lifted his eyes and
looked, and behold, three men were standing by him; and when he saw
them, he ran from the tent door to meet them, and bowed himself to the
ground, and said, "My Lord, if I have now found favor in Your sight, do
not pass on by Your servant. Please let a little water be brought, and wash
your feet, and rest yourselves under the tree. And I will bring a morsel
of bread, that you may refresh your hearts. After that you may pass by,
inasmuch as you have come to your servant."
They said, "Do as you have said."

—Genesis 18:1-5 (NKJV)

I find this passage fascinating! The thought that Abraham's
actions refreshed the heart of God, the Self-Existent One, completely arrests my heart! I want to refresh the heart of God too!

For me, this passage sparks two obvious questions, what does
it mean to "refresh" the heart of God, and how did Abraham do it?

First, what does it mean to "refresh His heart"? The Hebrew
word for refresh in this passage is *sa ad* (H5582) and it means

to sustain, support, strengthen, uphold, or comfort—and more specifically, to do so with food. This description reminds me of a meal I ate on a trip to Houston with close friends. We ate at a fancy restaurant with excellent service that served incredibly delicious farm-to-table food. When the meal was over, I felt completely satisfied and encouraged due to the combination of the meal, my friends, and the atmosphere. That is the picture that comes to mind when I read this description.

Second, how did Abraham do it? I think the answer is beautifully simple—Abraham responded to God. Abraham ran toward Him, bowed low, brought water for the men to wash their feet, and had a meal prepared.

Though we do not know for sure by reading the passage, I think it is safe to assume Abraham had been thinking about God. After all, God had just appeared to Abraham and told him he would be the father of many nations through a son named Isaac, which seemed impossible given his and Sarai's advanced age. I imagine Abraham had a lot to ponder! Then, amid his pondering, God appeared face-to-face.

Abraham was looking and pondering. Then Abraham saw God and recognized Him. Finally, Abraham responded by worshipping Him. Could it be that simple? Could our response to God refresh Him? Could our worship be the bread that leaves Him satisfied?

I know God does not need anything; however, the Bible does say it is good to praise Him, and His attention is on those who worship Him (Ps. 147 [AMP]).

Self-Reflection: May we be the ones who recognize and respond to Him when He comes. May we satisfy Him with our worship.

Prayer: Father—forgive me for making things about me so often. Too often, I am focused on myself, distracted by the world, and not looking for You. I know You are all around. Turn my heart entirely to You. Teach me how to worship in a way that honors You alone. Amen.

Daily Reading: Genesis 16–18

Graciously Remembered, Graciously Visited

*The Lord graciously remembered and visited Sarah as He had said,
and the Lord did for her as He had promised. So Sarah conceived and
gave birth to a son for Abraham in his old age, at the appointed time
of which God had spoken to him.*

—Genesis 21:1–2 (AMP)

I have a list of things I have been waiting on God to accomplish,
things He's promised in His Word, things He's spoken to my heart,
and desires deep within me I believe are from Him, and it is easy
to become weary in the waiting. Often, it is tempting to give up.

I think about Sarah and Abraham and how long they waited
for a child. Considering the culture in which they lived, it is likely
they were married well before age 20. If Abraham was 100 when
Isaac was born, they waited at least 80 years to conceive a child
of their own and fulfill their hearts' desire.

Then, when they had given up hope, there was a "suddenly of
God." The purposes and timing of God aligned for Abraham and
Sarah, and they bore a son. Adonai, the Eternal One, graciously
remembered Sarah, and at His appointed time, He visited her and
accomplished all He promised He would.

Self-Reflection: This passage encourages me deeply to hold on, press in, and not give up. In time, He will accomplish all that He promised He would. In the meantime, He is positioning and preparing me to carry the promises He has put in my heart. Likewise, He positions and prepares my children to fulfill His will for their lives. His plan and His promise in His timing, not mine, so I can stop worrying and trying to control things. He is good. His leadership in my life is perfect, and He can be trusted.

Prayer: Father—forgive me for trying to control and manipulate the timing of things and situations. Help me to trust You, Your timing, and Your perfect plan for myself and my family. Graciously remember and visit me in Your perfect time. I want to be near Your heart in the waiting—draw me close, reposition me, and prepare me. Thank you for loving me. Amen.

Daily Reading: Genesis 19–21

BEHOLD HIM

*Now it was after these things that God tested Abraham. He said to him,
"Abraham." "Hineni," he said." . . .But the angel of Adonai called to
him from heaven and said, "Abraham! Abraham!" He said, "Hineni!"
Then He said, "Do not reach out your hand against the young man—
do nothing to him at all. For now I know that you are one who fears
God—you did not withhold your son, your only son, from Me."*

—Genesis 22:1, 11–12 (TLV)

There is much to say about God testing Abraham, the three-day
journey of carrying the wood and the fire, Abraham's absolute
trust and confidence in God's provision, the subsequent binding
of Isaac, and ultimately Abraham offering Isaac as a sacrifice.
We all know how the story ends and the imagery foretelling of
the coming Messiah; however, what fascinates me about the
passage is how it began.

Abraham's test starts and ends with one word: *hineni* (H2009).

The Hebrew word used in these two verses means
"behold me."

To behold something means to look or gaze at it intently
with great appreciation. The word comes from an Old English
compound meaning to give great regard to, or to hold in view,

and was later used to describe keeping, possessing, or protecting something.

Abraham's greatest test started and ended with him gazing intently at the sovereign God of the Universe. Both times, God called Abraham by name to get his attention and said, Behold me! See me!

Once Abraham *beheld* the One True God, Elohim, and truly *saw* Him, the test paled in comparison.

Self-Reflection: Whatever test I am facing, whatever He is asking of me, it pales in comparison with the One True God of the Universe. May He find me faithful, may He find my gaze upon Him, and may I hear His voice when He calls me to gaze at and behold Him.

Prayer: Father—too often, the noise drowns out Your voice. Give me ears to hear Your voice above all things. Give me eyes to see and truly behold You. Be exalted above all other things in my life and my affections. Amen.

Daily Reading: Genesis 22–24

The Promise Keeper

"Dwell in this land, and I will be with you and bless you; for to you and your descendants I give all these lands, and I will perform the oath which I swore to Abraham your father. And I will make your descendants multiply as the stars of heaven; I will give to your descendants all these lands; and in your seed all the nations of the earth shall be blessed."

—Genesis 26:3-4 (NKJV)

And the Lord appeared to him the same night and said, "I am the God of your father Abraham; do not fear, for I am with you. I will bless you and multiply your descendants for My servant Abraham's sake."

—Genesis 26:24 (NKJV)

Isaac was in line to receive the promise God made to Abraham because of God's faithfulness alone. Isaac could not, nor did he have to earn it; it was a promise God alone would and could fulfill. When God made the covenant with Abraham in Genesis 15 and 17, God did not give an "out" or a list of requirements. God is not fickle like that. We break promises and relationships easily, but God is the original Promise Keeper. He is not a man who would lie (Num. 29:13), and He will fulfill His purposes (Lam. 2:17).

One more thing stands out to me in this passage—the idea of generational callings. I believe there are generational blessings and callings. Years ago, my husband's grandmother, Grandma Trixie Purtell, told me that she prayed for many years for someone in her lineage to have what she felt was her gift and calling—the ability to pick up any instrument, play it, and lead others in worship. She explained that while some of the children and grandchildren could play and most definitely sing, she believed her great-grandson, our son, Randal, was an answer to her prayers. It is easy to see that the Purtell family is musically and pastorally inclined. Some of the grandsons preach, one son-in-law is a pastor, and all five of her kids sing incredibly well and play instruments. Several other great-grandchildren are also musically gifted. Simply put, music and ministry are in the Purtell blood. Music, worship, and ministry are a generational blessing and calling on the Purtell lineage. And we are not unique! I know many families, specifically the family of my mentor, Pastor Olen, who are full of pastors and ministers. The generational calling on their family is obvious!

Self-Reflection: May we be encouraged to look to Him to help us identify His plan and call for our family, ever mindful that He will keep His word. God keeps His Word and His promises to us because He is just that good!

Prayer: Father, open my eyes to see the generational blessings I am blind to. Thank you for placing me here for such a time as this. Help me to trust Your plan and Your timing. I am impatient, but I know You will come, keep Your Word, and fulfill Your purposes for my life when it's time. Amen.

Daily Reading: Genesis 25–26

HE SEES

Leah's eyes were delicate, but Rachel was beautiful of form and appearance.... When the Lord saw that Leah was unloved, He opened her womb; but Rachel was barren.

—Genesis 29:17, 31 (NKJV)

Leah was nothing special to look at according to the description above. The Hebrew word for "delicate" in the passage above, rakot, means soft, tender, or gentle. Rabbinic sources teach that she either had a physical impairment or her eyes were tender and delicate from constant crying. Regardless of which teaching is true, something wounded her. She knew rejection well.

Then God saw that Leah was śānē (H8130). The translation above uses the word "unloved," but I'm not sure that's strong enough. The word śānē means to be seen as a foe or enemy or to be hated or despised. Leah was hated and rejected.

Then God rā'â Leah. By Hebrew translation, He considered, noticed, looked upon, and beheld her. He *saw* her when others did not.

Leah. One rejected my man, now *seen* by Jehovah God.

And when God saw Leah, He opened her womb, transforming

her through the birthing process as she moved from affliction and rejection to hope of being seen and finally to praise.

Self-Reflection: What if God is using the rejection and pain of this world to birth praise in and through me? I am encouraged and reminded that God sees me, He has not forgotten me, and He is birthing praise in and through me.

Prayer: Abba, thank You for loving me. Thank You for seeing me. I have been angry and hurt over rejection by men. Help me look to You alone for comfort, acceptance, and love. You see the brokenhearted. You provide all that I need. You are good. Your leadership in my life is perfect, and You can be trusted. Amen.

Daily Reading: Genesis 27–29

THE FEAR OF ISAAC

"Unless the God of my father, the God of Abraham and the Fear of Isaac, had been with me, surely now you would have sent me away empty-handed. God has seen my affliction and the labor of my hands, and rebuked you last night.... [Laban spoke] The God of Abraham, the God of Nahor, and the God of their father judge between us." And Jacob swore by the Fear of his father Isaac.

—Genesis 31:42, 53 (NKJV)

But Jacob swore [only] by [the one true God] the Fear of his father Isaac.

—Genesis 31:53 (AMP)

People use many different names to describe the character of the One True God, and in this passage, I learned a new one that is used only twice in the Bible (both times are in this chapter): the Fear of Isaac.

While studying several commentaries, I learned that many practiced idolatry in Jacob's lineage—Terah, Abraham, Nahor, and Leban. However, there was one who did not—his father, Isaac.

At this point in Jacob's story, he *knew* about God, but he didn't *know* God personally, and even though Jacob only knew *of* and *about* God, Jacob feared Him. There was something about growing up as Isaac's son, perhaps something Isaac did, said, or lived out before Jacob, which caused Jacob to know and fear God. Jacob knew that his father, Isaac, truly feared the True God, and even though Jacob did not fully understand it, Jacob feared God, too, and swore an oath to His name alone.

This thought process has led me to wonder about our impact on the lives of those we influence and lead, specifically our children, friends, and those in our community. Am I living my faith in such a way that it clearly points to the One True God as Isaac did? Does my love point to Him? Do my choices and words exalt Him? Am I making Him, the One True Eternal God, obvious to others through my words, deeds, and actions, or do my words, deeds, and actions cause others to close their eyes to Him? Everything we do and everything we say either exalts God or exalts Satan. We either praise and magnify God or we praise and magnify the enemy. There is no middle ground or gray area. How I respond to and live my faith before my children and those I encounter daily has an eternal impact.

Self-Reflection: At the end of the day, we must choose to either walk with Him or be apart from Him; therefore, may others see in me a reflection of God that draws them to Him rather than repels them.

Prayer: Father, forgive me for where and how I have misrepresented You. You are perfect, and You are good. Help me live in integrity before You so others may see You clearly in and through my life. Amen.

Daily Reading: Genesis 30–31

FORGIVENESS
AND RECONCILIATION

But Esau ran to meet him and embraced him, and hugged his neck and kissed him, and they wept [for joy].

—Genesis 33:4 (AMP)

Esau was bitter (Gen. 27:34), hated his brother, and threatened to kill him (Gen. 27:41). Jacob escaped, and they were apart for twenty years. Then, when Jacob finally returned, Esau forgave him—completely.

I have been pondering what must have happened in Esau's heart to move him from hate to forgiveness during those twenty years apart. What led Esau to run, embrace and kiss Jacob, and weep for joy? It was not the lavish gifts Jacob sent—so what could it have been? We know Jacob's story but not Esau's—the one I am so curious about.

First—Esau was blessed by God. When Jacob offered his lavish gifts, Esau first refused them, stating he had enough (Gen. 33:9). Could Esau have been more focused on his present blessings than the past deceit? Second—Esau responded. When

Jacob took the first step (Gen. 32:1–6) and sent a messenger ahead to ask for *ḥēn*—a Hebrew word that means "grace"—Esau responded immediately and headed to meet his brother. Could it be that Esau had already forgiven Jacob?

Esau's actions—embracing Jacob, kissing him, and weeping over him—are all actions that spoke of complete acceptance and forgiveness at that time. Something radical happened in Esau's heart to bring him to the point of completely forgiving Jacob long before Jacob headed home.

How many times have I thought I had forgiven someone for the deep pain they caused me only to realize I was still holding on to a wound, a hurt, or an offense when I saw them again? Too many to count.

Esau stood ready to forgive. Jacob moved toward him and asked for grace. Esau readily responded with forgiveness. The reality is reconciliation would not have happened without both people. Esau was ready to forgive, but they would have never reconciled if Jacob hadn't gone home. Whether we find ourselves in Esau's shoes or Jacob's, we each play a part in the reconciliation and healing of relationships.

Self-Reflection: Be like Esau. Deal with hurts, lay down offense, and stand ready. Be like Jacob. Ask for grace and offer restitution. Then, come together, let go of the pain and the past, embrace and accept one another completely, and experience the joy of true forgiveness.

Prayer: Father—you know my heart's deep desire for reconciliation and healing. Help me to find peace like Esau and stand ready to forgive. Give me the courage to ask for grace where needed and offer restitution. Heal our hearts and restore the years the locusts have eaten. Amen.

Daily Reading: Genesis 32–34

DREAM A LITTLE DREAM

Then he dreamed still another dream and told it to his brothers, and said, "Look, I have dreamed another dream. And this time, the sun, the moon, and the eleven stars bowed down to me." So he told it to his father and his brothers; and his father rebuked him and said to him, "What is this dream that you have dreamed? Shall your mother and I and your brothers indeed come to bow down to the earth before you?" And his brothers envied him, but his father kept the matter in mind.

—Genesis 37:9-11 (NKJV)

I still remember the first dream Randal shared with me that awakened me to the idea of God speaking to me and to him in a creative way.

"Mommy! I fly up in a big, yellow plane, and I fly around and around and drop presents to people on the ground!"

"That's cool," I replied, only half listening to my then three-year-old while I got breakfast ready.

Then, the next day, he had the same dream about the yellow plane dropping the same presents to the same people on the ground—this time I paid attention. I thought about it throughout our morning routine, and when I finally had time alone with the Lord, I asked Him about it. His response was simply "Pay attention."

Dream interpretation was not new to me. I'd taken some classes at our church, Shady Grove, so I dusted off my handy little book to look up symbols: planes can symbolize prophetic things, vehicles represent ministry or calling, and presents suggest spiritual gifts.

After praying, I believed God began speaking about a calling on Randal's life. So I prayed, treasured it in my heart, and recorded it in a journal. More dreams came, and years later, after church one day, Randal told us he felt called to be a "worshipping missionary" who sang about the holiness of God and taught people how to worship. What he heard confirmed what God started speaking years earlier.

Self-Reflection: I have been asked over the years how we raised worshippers. While we did many small, intentional things over the years, teaching them to hear God's voice for themselves was the most critical thing—and one way He speaks is through dreams and visions.

Prayer: Father, thank You that You still speak today! Give me ears to hear and a heart to receive Your word. Give me the wisdom to understand what You want to say through my dreams and the wisdom to encourage and train the arrows You entrusted to me. Help me follow Your voice alone. Amen.

Daily Reading: Genesis 35–37

FAVOR

The Lord was with Joseph, and he was a successful man; and he was in the house of his master the Egyptian. And his master saw that the Lord was with him and that the Lord made all he did to prosper in his hand. So Joseph found favor in his sight, and served him. Then he made him overseer of his house, and all that he had he put under his authority.

—Genesis 39:2-4 (NKJV)

But the Lord was with Joseph and showed him mercy, and He gave him favor in the sight of the keeper of the prison. The keeper of the prison did not look into anything that was under Joseph's authority, because the Lord was with him; and whatever he did, the Lord made it prosper.

—Genesis 39:21, 23 (NKJV)

Favor.

By definition, favor means friendly regard shown toward another, especially by a superior or gracious kindness. The word is derived from the Latin word *favere*, meaning to show kindness to someone, and from the French word *fovere*, which means to cherish.

Favor.

Goodness, it is a beautiful word and an incredible experience.

But the truth about favor is this: it cannot be "earned." Favor is a gift that comes from God alone. Sure, people may show us favor, but according to what I read about Joseph, both Potiphar and the Prison Guard showed Joseph favor because God was with him, showed him mercy and kindness, and made everything he did prosper.

God's favor is with us because *He* is *good*. He is merciful, gracious, and kind—and He loves us! The story of Joseph encourages me because Joseph experienced God's favor in a difficult season. Sold as an enslaved person and taken far from his home, Joseph, the most beloved son of his father, was enslaved to Potiphar, yet through it all, God was with him and gave him favor. Then, when it seemed things could not get any worse, Joseph found himself in a dark prison, wrongly accused, and experienced even more favor.

God's favor rested on Joseph in the absolute darkest, most hopeless environment. Likewise, His favor rests on me in my darkest, most desperate, hopeless moments.

Self-Reflection: When my heart is weary, my thoughts wander, and I am tempted to lose hope, may I be ever mindful of the favor that rests upon me, His beloved, cherished daughter.

Prayer: Father—you know the deep anxiety and fear in my heart, the temptation I feel right now to fall into despair. I cry out to You for mercy. You see me now. You know what I need and what's before me. Though man's favor may pass away and fade, Your favor is for a lifetime. When others forsake or forget me, You are near and will be with me no matter what happens. You are good. You can be trusted. Your leadership in my life is perfect. Help me to rest in your truth. Amen.

Daily Reading: Genesis 38–40

HURRY!
CHANGE YOUR CLOTHES!

Then Pharaoh sent and called for Joseph, and they hurriedly brought him out of the dungeon; and when Joseph shaved himself and changed his clothes [making himself presentable], he came to Pharaoh.

—Genesis 41:14 (AMP)

Two long years in a dark prison cell. Prisons then were not like prisons today. Imagine a cellar, deep in the ground, hewn in by clay and rocks, smelling worse than the worst bathroom you have ever entered. The walls are wet. Bugs abound. Excrement coats the corners. Darkness takes on a new meaning. Joseph had two long years there—then suddenly, it was over!

Joseph had a "suddenly of God." The timing of God and the purposes of God intersected, and Joseph experienced a suddenly of God!

Then, after leaving the dungeon cell, the first thing Joseph did was to make himself presentable. He washed, he shaved, and—this part leaped off the page at me—he changed his clothes.

We know how the rest of the story unfolds—but something resonated in my heart over Joseph changing his clothes and leaving them behind! The pit was the place of preparation. It was where Joseph's character was refined and tested for the position Pharaoh would place him in. Likewise, we all experience seasons of "death to self"—where our character is refined and defined amid great adversity so that we are ready to walk in His calling for us.

The new position brought forth a new identity and radical provision. Suddenly, Joseph was given a new name. Suddenly, he became second-in-command. Suddenly, he was given a wife, and later he had two sons. He led through excess and scarcity. God positioned Joseph to be a blessing and accomplish His purposes. Likewise, God has a "suddenly" for each of us. Get ready for some new garments.

Self-Reflection: May we see the seasons of adversity as seasons of refining, preparation, and positioning. When we are called up out of the pit of despair and preparation, may we leave our "garments" of the past behind. May we leave behind the pain and the "excrement" of the season of affliction. Sure, tears may come, but we, like Joseph, have been given new clothes! Stop trying to put on old, stinky garments!

Prayer: Father—your leadership is perfect. I do not understand seasons of affliction, nor do I like them. But—I understand they are necessary training grounds for my heart. I yield my heart to you. Position me and prepare me to live an unoffended life before You. You are good, and You can be trusted. Amen.

Daily Reading: Genesis 41–42

GOD SENT ME

*"So now, don't be grieved and don't be angry in your own eyes that you
sold me here—since it was for preserving life that God sent me here before
you...But God sent me ahead of you to ensure a remnant in the land and
to keep you alive for a great escape. So now, it wasn't you, you didn't send
me here, but God!"*

—Genesis 45:5, 7-8 (TLV)

The Hebrew word used to describe what Joseph's brothers did
to him, *shâlak*, is very similar to the word used when Joseph
spoke to his brothers—*shâlach*.

Joseph's brothers "took him and *threw* him into the pit."
(Gen. 37:24). The Hebrew word *shâlak* in this passage is a
primitive root word and means to throw out, to throw down,
or to throw away; to cast (away, down, forth, off, out), hurl, or
pluck; or an adventure.

Then, three times, Joseph told his brothers, "God *shâlach*
me." The Hebrew *shâlach* means to send away, to send for, or
to send out. Could Joseph be emphasizing each meaning of the
word? God sent me away. God sent for me. God sent me out.

I do not know Hebrew, but when I realized only one letter
separated "being cast away" from "being sent," I wanted to
shout! Wow!

Joseph's perspective shifted somewhere between being cast into a pit and being made second-in-command to Pharaoh. Being "cast off" became an adventure, and the adventure led to fulfilling God's plan to preserve their lineage.

One letter. One choice. Being thrown aside or being sent. The space between "tossed aside" and "sent" is small.

Self-Reflection: Perhaps what we feel and what looks impossible from our view in the pit is the beginning of an adventure of God sending and positioning us to accomplish His purposes, not ours. May Your will be done, God, not mine. Life with You is a great adventure.

Prayer: Father—forgive me for complaining when You have been positioning me. It's uncomfortable and scary. Help me to see it as an adventure and to receive all You are doing with gratitude. Help me to shift my perspective. It seems small, but it feels so big. You are good. You can be trusted. Your leadership in my life is perfect. Amen.

Daily Reading: Genesis 43–45

SETTLED IN THE BEST

Moreover, they said to Pharaoh, "We have come to live temporarily
(sojourn) in the land [of Egypt], for there is no pasture for the flocks of
your servants [in our land], for the famine is very severe in Canaan. So
now, please let your servants live in the land of Goshen." Then Pharaoh
spoke to Joseph, saying, "Your father and your brothers have come to you.
The land of Egypt is before you; settle your father and your brothers in the
best of the land. Let them live in the land of Goshen; and if you know of
any men of ability among them, put them in charge of my livestock."

—Genesis 47:4-6 (AMP)

Now [the people of] Israel lived in the country of Egypt, in [the land of]
Goshen, and they gained possessions and acquired property there and were
fruitful and multiplied greatly.

—Genesis 47:27 (AMP)

When Jacob and his sons, along with their wives and children,
finally arrived at their "temporary" home in Egypt, Pharaoh told
Joseph to "settle [them] in the best of the land," and they were
greatly blessed there. Jacob's family went from severe famine
to the best of the land and was greatly blessed.

Wait. Think about that for a few seconds and let that sink in: from severe famine to being settled in the best land to being greatly blessed.

There was a real, physical famine across the land. Jacob didn't know how he would provide or what they would eat—and he had a lot of mouths to feed! But—God *knew*! God had a plan that He had been working on for a long time!

Years before the famine, God sent Joseph to prepare a place and a way to save his family. Joseph went through a personal famine. He experienced devastating loss, and he experienced great blessings. He was prepared to help settle his family and position them for blessing.

When things were bleak and hopeless, God provided, through Pharaoh, the best land for Jacob's family to settle in—and there, they prospered. Again, we see the "suddenly" of God—when His timing and His plan intersect.

As I look back over some seasons that were "famines" in our lives, I can now see clearly how God settled us in "the best land" and "greatly blessed" us. While it's hard and sometimes impossible to see, while it rips our hearts out and we feel flooded with desperation in the place of severe famine, I am fully confident that He is moving, positioning, and settling us—and He will bless us.

Self-Reflection: All of us experience these seasons. It's not unique to me or you. Perhaps He's using a famine in our lives to reposition us. Maybe He's settling us in a new place to bless others and to be blessed. Whatever season you are in personally, and whatever season those dear to you are in, may we all find hope in the knowledge that He loves us, and He has a plan for us. May we embrace those who are suffering with kindness and grace.

Prayer: Father—help me to trust Your plan. Forgive me for my doubt. Give me grace for those in need and who are hurting. You are good. Your way is perfect. Your leadership in my life is perfect, and You can be trusted. Amen.

Daily reading: Genesis 46–47

MY SHEPHERD

*Then Jacob (Israel) blessed Joseph, and said, "The God before whom my
fathers Abraham and Isaac walked [in faithful obedience], The God who
has been my Shepherd [leading and caring for me] all my life to this day,
The Angel [that is, the Lord Himself] who has redeemed me [continually]
from all evil, Bless the boys; and may my name live on in them [may they
be worthy of having their names linked with mine]."*

—Genesis 48:15-6 (AMP)

I tried to pay attention in these chapters to how Jacob referred
to and "named" God. He called God the Fear of Isaac twice,
and several times he called Him the God of My Father, Isaac,
and the God of Abraham. But here, at the end of his life, He
refers to God as *his* Shepherd. It becomes personal and intimate.

A shepherd protects, positions, and provides for his sheep. He
walks among them. When they are in danger, he moves them to
safety. When one is lost, he finds and restores it to the fold. He
gathers them at night. He leads them to water and food.

A sheep *knows* the Shepherd's voice because they have spent
time together in both adversity and abundance. The sheep heard
the Shepherd's voice repeatedly as he called their name, directed
them, and maybe even sang to them.

The point is this: at the end of his life, Jacob recognized and used a personal name for the One he used to call the Fear of Isaac and the God of his fathers Abraham and Isaac.

God desires to get personal with us, no matter what it takes. He will use every opportunity to draw us close to Him. He waits patiently for us when we wander. He calls out to us when we are lost and in a pit. He picks us up when we are wounded. He wants us to know Him personally and intimately, to know and see Him as the One who cares for us above all others.

Self-Reflection: God is my Shepherd. Is He yours too?

Prayer: Good Shepherd—forgive me for my wandering. Thank you for rescuing me more than I realize. Thank you for protecting and guiding me. Thank you for providing for me. Your leadership in my life is perfect. You are good, and You can be trusted—through the good and the bad—and my heart knows that fully. Give me ears to hear Your voice and a heart to respond quickly. Amen.

Daily Reading: Genesis 48–50

ENCOUNTER: A HOLY FLAME

Then the angel of Adonai appeared to him in a flame of fire from within a bush. So he looked and saw the bush burning with fire, yet it was not consumed. Moses thought, "I will go now, and see this great sight. Why is the bush not burnt?" When Adonai saw that he turned to look, He called to him out of the midst of the bush and said, "Moses, Moses!" So he answered, "Hineni." Then He said, "Come no closer. Take your sandals off your feet, for the place where you are standing is holy ground." Moreover He said, "I am the God of your father, the God of Abraham, Isaac and Jacob." So Moses hid his face, because he was afraid to look at God.

—Exodus 3:2-6 (TLV)

I clearly remember my second visit to Shady Grove Church in Grand Prairie, Texas, and my first "encounter." Years earlier, I had visited with a friend to attend a concert and promptly walked out when I saw people lying on the floor. It was not for me.

Fast-forward six years when I returned a second time with a different friend, but this time broken, abused, and divorced. As the music started, people all around me sang at the top of their lungs in complete abandonment. I had never seen this in the churches I grew up in. The songs were simple, repeating the identical stanzas multiple times, and as the music lingered,

I began to sing and suddenly found myself on my knees, face to the ground, weeping. There was something in this place—Someone present that I did not know yet—that fascinated me, and just like Moses, curiosity and wonder had me turning to behold the flame in the bush. The encounter marked me and forever changed my destiny.

I grew up in church. I knew the old hymns and heard plenty of three-point sermons with great alliteration. But my "experiences" at church didn't change me. Experiences result from things that happen to you or a skill you get by doing something. My "experiences" at church affected my thoughts but nothing else. It took an encounter to change my heart.

Encounters happen when we meet someone or something unexpectedly. I believe that is what happened to me on my second visit to Shady Grove; I had an encounter, an unexpected meeting with God that was so different it captured my attention.

That is also what happened to Moses. The Lord wanted to get his attention because He had an assignment for Moses, a calling, if you will, so He arranged a meeting of chance, something unexpected—a flame in the midst of a bush—and the flame did not destroy it!

A flame that did not consume had to evoke curiosity! The flame of fire was going against what Moses knew to be true, an experience that says fires are destructive! But Moses encountered the Flame that purified, that made the place "holy ground."

I remember a time in 2021 when I was captivated by fires that dotted the landscape as I drove through Flint Hills, Kansas, close to midnight. I have no idea how many fires were burning—but as I scanned the horizon, I turned off the music, slowed down, and felt the peace of God enter my car. It was a holy moment for me—an encounter with Him. Range burning is a long-standing practice of Kansas ranchers used to enhance and improve their soil, strengthen native grasses, and destroy weeds. In a way, they use fire to purify and cleanse their land. Likewise, could an encounter with God be like the Kansas range burnings, meant to purify and strengthen us, to get our attention so He can remove that which does not need to be there?

Perhaps. Perhaps not. But either way, He's trying to get our attention. May we have eyes to see, ears to hear, and a ready yes on our lips when He comes to encounter us.

Self-Reflection: I believe God desires to encounter us—to move us beyond what our finite mind understands based on our experiences with the programs and plans of man—to a life-changing, life-altering encounter that marks us for eternity.

Prayer: Father—thank You for pursuing me. Thank You for never giving up on me. Thank You for waiting until I turned to You. Your leadership is perfect. You are good, and You can be trusted. Prepare my heart for all You have for me. Amen.

Daily Reading: Exodus 1–3

NOW GO!

Then Moses said to the Lord, "Please, Lord, I am not a man of words (eloquent, fluent), neither before nor since You have spoken to Your servant; for I am slow of speech and tongue." The Lord said to him, "Who has made man's mouth? Or who makes the mute or the deaf, or the seeing or the blind? Is it not I, the Lord? Now then go, and I, even I, will be with your mouth, and will teach you what you shall say." But he said, "Please my Lord, send the message [of rescue to Israel] by [someone else,] whomever else You will [choose]." Then the anger of the Lord was kindled and burned against Moses.

—Exodus 4:10-14 (AMP)

Sometimes I feel like Moses—slow of speech, at a loss for words, fearful and uncertain—especially in the heat of the moment.

How many times have I responded to God like Moses? He gives a directive, and I reply with hesitation and uncertainty, questioning my ability.

Pastor Olen, my mentor and spiritual father, relayed a message to me that he heard by Joy Dawson once with three simple steps to walking in obedience to God:

1. Do the first thing God tells you to do,
2. Do the next thing God tells you to do, and
3. Do the next thing God tells you to do.

It sounds simple, yet my fear often derails me. Many scientists and educators now believe there are just two primary emotions and from them stem all others: fear and love. If that is true, then perhaps my love for Him can be stronger than the fear that leads to disobedience because the last thing I want to do is kindle His anger against me.

Self-Reflection: In 1 John 4:18 we read that perfect love casts out all fear. May His love be louder than all the internal noise that keeps us from responding with a resounding *yes* to what He asks of us.

Prayer: Father—how often I've listened to fear. Forgive me for giving space to fear. Perfect Your love in my heart. May my love for You be my loudest yes. Amen.

Daily Reading: Exodus 4–6

JUST A FINGER

Then the magicians said to Pharaoh, "This is the finger of God."
But Pharaoh's heart grew hard, and he did not heed them, just as
the Lord had said.

—Exodus 8:19 (NKJV)

It only took three plagues for the magicians to recognize the power of God.

We study the plagues annually during Passover, and based on what I can surmise, God sent the ten plagues for two primary reasons—first, judgment against those who oppressed His people and refused to repent, and second, to show His power, His power to save and His power above all of the Egyptian gods. All ten plagues were directed to the various gods the Egyptians worshipped. And, as an interesting note, 10 is the number of completion.

The magicians duplicated the first two plagues with their sorcery—but after the third, even they recognized the supernatural power of God in just His *finger*! It didn't take them long. Then, even some of Pharaoh's own servants began to believe after the seventh plague (Exod. 9:20).

How often do we *see* the power of God at work and deny Him? He is gracious to come to us over and over—patiently pursuing us—clearly showing His power above all others—giving us opportunities to repent and obey.

God may not send plagues to us now like He did then, but I have experienced, more than once, how miserable it is to delay obedience.

God is more powerful than anything we face and anything happening to us. He is greater than our disobedience and doubts. He is exalted over our fear and our past—no matter how battered and no matter how broken. I am proof that He is bigger.

Self-Reflection: May we find rest in Him, knowing that our God is able to fight any battle before us. If He, by merely His finger, could defeat the Egyptian gods, just imagine the protection, security, and provision that comes from being positioned under His wing (Ps. 91)!

Prayer: Father, thank you for Your provision and protection. Thank You for showing us a better way. Help me to trust You in the battles I face. Many I love are facing battles—give them grace and strengthen their hearts. Draw them close. You are good. Your leadership is perfect, and You can be trusted. Amen.

Daily Reading: Exodus 7–9

FOR THEIR SAKE

*And that you may tell in the hearing of your son and your son's son the
mighty things I have done in Egypt, and My signs which I have done
among them, that you may know that I am the Lord.*

—Exodus 10:2 (NKJV)

*"And that you may recount and explain in the hearing of your son, and
your grandson, what I have done [repeatedly] to make a mockery of
the Egyptians—My signs [of divine power] which I have done among
them—so that you may know [without any doubt] and recognize
[clearly] that I am the Lord."*

—Exodus 10:2 (AMP)

Anyone who knows us well knows that more than anything
we want our children to be worshippers of God and most of
our decisions and actions are enacted with that in mind. One
of the intentional things we have done over the years to teach
them about God has been to observe Shabbat and many of the
Jewish feasts—not because we are Jewish, but because we love
the God they do, and we learn about Him through observing
the feasts. And Passover—as somber as it is—is my favorite
next to Shabbat.

Pharaoh and the Egyptians received plagues—*maaggêphâh* (divine judgments)—from God, but the Israelites received *'ôwth*—signs and miracles—as pledges or attestations of divine presence.

Our deliverance may look different in the present day than it did for the Israelites, but He still delivers, and He still performs miracles on our behalf. Remember, His delays are not denials, and His no is often a "not yet," sometimes it simply isn't time yet.

Part of my responsibility as a mom is to share signs and wonders with my children—to testify to His provision and goodness—so that they can get to know Him and His character. Psalms 78 says that one generation shall tell the next of the mighty deeds of God so that they (the next generation) will not be stubborn and stiff-necked (Marci's summary).

From the beginning of time, family was part of God's plan. He wants us to tell our children and grandchildren, nieces and nephews, and the almost-mines about Him. He wants us to testify of Him! It's part of His plan!

Self-Reflection: Now isn't the time to be silent. May we have courage and boldness to be witnesses of God and His goodness to those around us. May our words and actions point others to Him. For their sake, I will not be silent. For their sake, I will tell the mighty things He has done.

Prayer: Father—thank you! Thank you for our family and for another opportunity. Forgive me for when I've complained about your delays and denials. Help me to see Your hand at work repositioning and preparing. You are good. Your leadership in my life is perfect, and You can be trusted. Amen.

Daily Reading: Exodus 10–12

TWO PILLARS

And the Lord went before them by day in a pillar of cloud to lead the way, and by night in a pillar of fire to give them light, so as to go by day and night. He did not take away the pillar of cloud by day or the pillar of fire by night from before the people.

— Exodus 13:21-22 (NKJV)

Off they go—being led through the wilderness, the long way, by a pillar of cloud before them and a pillar of fire behind them, *the* physical, tangible, visible presence of God going before and behind them! Something about the imagery gives me great comfort!

As a Texan, I know the relief from clouds on a hot summer day. I also know the comfort a fire brings on cold winter days. A cloud by day, something they could see and look to, something to hide them, and something to comfort them, and a fire by night, something to light their way, something to warm them, and something to hide them.

The imagery reminds me of what God spoke to my heart regarding Psalms 23: a shepherd provides for His sheep, protects His sheep, and positions His sheep. God used the cloud to hide the Israelites from Pharaoh and the Egyptians, and from the pillars of cloud and fire, He brought trouble and confusion to the Egyptians (Exod. 14:19–24). He positioned and protected His people and provided a way of escape. His presence remained with them day and night. He was a good, fierce Shepherd to them.

Self-Reflection: The Bible says that God is a rewarder of those who diligently seek Him (Heb. 11:6), that He longs to be gracious to us (Isa. 30:18), and that His ears are attentive to our prayers (Ps. 34:15). Whatever we face, may we rest in knowing deep in our hearts that God stands before us ready to protect us and to lead the way and God stands behind us to comfort us and to light the way; we only need to hold our peace and follow His voice.

Prayer: Father, help me trust in Your voice. Forgive me when I've stepped outside of the protection of Your presence. Guide me and protect me. Make the way clear. You are good. You can be trusted, and Your leadership in my life is perfect. Amen.

Daily Reading: Exodus 13–15

SHABBAT: A HOLY GIFT

But he said to them, "This is what Adonai has said. Tomorrow is a
Shabbat rest, a holy Shabbat to Adonai. Bake whatever you would bake,
and boil what you would boil. Store up for yourselves everything that
remains, to be kept until the morning."...So the people rested on the
seventh day.

—Exodus 16:23, 30 (TLV)

Shabbâth—perhaps from the Assyrian word šabattum, meaning
a day of rest of heart and an intensive form of shâbath (cease,
celebrate, rest).

Shabbat. It is a holy gift and our favorite family time.

This verse is special to me because it's the first time in the
Bible that God commanded His people to observe Shabbat and
He provided a way for them—He sent a double portion. All I
know about Shabbat I learned from author and friend Bonnie
Wilks through her book *Sabbath: A Gift of Time*. I first heard
about Shabbat through our church, but when I read her book, I
finally understood the Sabbath was for me. She teaches in her
book that God created the sabbath for all mankind (Gen. 2:2–3).
Rest is God's idea.

When we began observing Shabbat, something shifted in
me and our home. He made a way for us to rest and connect.

"Unplugging" is His design and plan for us. He desires that we pause, reflect, rest, and remember.

When we light our candles on Friday, we do so to remember what He brought us through that week and to remind us to rest from the weariness of the week. We choose to incorporate many of the traditional Jewish elements because they are like memorial stones used to remember and exalt Him over our week—the hand washing, the cup, the bread, all of it.

I love etymology, and the first lines above revealed something new to me. The word Shabbat is perhaps from the Assyrian word šabattum, meaning day of rest of heart. That might be my new favorite meaning.

Self-Reflection: The encouragement and reminder for me is this: Rest. Pause. Reflect. Remember. Give thanks. Celebrate. He designed rest for our hearts. It is a holy gift. A gift like no other that I hope we can each open in our own way as we pause and rest from the weariness of the week so that we can reflect, remember, and celebrate all that He's done for us.

Prayer: Father, thank you for Bonnie and her family for opening this gift for me. Bless them. Thank You for Your provision of rest. I receive it. I am grateful. You are good. Your leadership in my life is perfect, and You can be trusted. Amen.

Daily Reading: Exodus 16–18

HONOR'S REWARD

"Honor [respect, obey, care for] your father and your mother, so that your days may be prolonged in the land the Lord your God gives you."

— Exodus 20:12 (AMP)

I have a few go-to, must-read-and-reread books—and *Honors Reward* by John Bevere is one of them. I read it in a season when I was serving on staff at Shady Grove Church as the founding pastor's assistant, and it revolutionized how I approached people.

Honoring someone means holding that person in high regard because of who they are and/or their position. Personally, I believe I am to honor everyone I encounter and treat them in an honorable way simply because all life comes from God alone.

Honoring others starts at home. How we treat, talk to, and respond to each other, our parents, our spouses, and even our children, teaches those in our home and under our influence how to respond, treat, and talk to others. Do we use kind words, or are we critical? Do we truly listen, or do we constantly interrupt? Do we give a soft answer or a harsh one? And when I'm the one mistreated, how do I respond? It is not easy—but it is my choice. Honor depends entirely upon me.

People may have dishonorable actions, but that does not mean I must respond dishonorably. People may yell, but I can choose a soft answer. People may mistreat me, but I can choose to respond kindly and set a boundary to protect myself in the future. It is important to me to raise kind kids who honor other humans, and it starts by modeling a life that honors others before them while setting boundaries and having healthy discussions when they disagree.

Self-Reflection: When we returned to Texas, we lived on the same property as my in-laws for six years. Our primary reason for staying there so long was to honor them. Then, we moved to my parents' house for a year. We have moved a lot, and a desire to honor God was always behind each move. He put it on our hearts when and where to move, and we followed. And the reward for honor? When I honor my parents and others, I can be assured of His protection: "'Honor your father and your mother just as Adonai your God commanded you, *so that your days may be long and it may go well with you in the land Adonai your God is giving you*'" (Deut: 5:16 [TLV])

Prayer: Father—help me to honor those around me. Help me to honor my family through word, action, and deed. Help me to walk faithfully to the land that You've called us to because You are good, You can be trusted, and Your leadership in my life is perfect. Amen.

Daily Reading: Exodus 19–21

THE ONLY ONE

"You shall not bow down to worship their gods, nor serve them, nor do [anything] in accordance with their practices. You shall completely overthrow them and break down their [sacred] pillars and images [of pagan worship]. You shall serve [only] the Lord your God, and He shall bless your bread and water. I will also remove sickness from among you.... You shall not make a covenant with them or with their gods. They shall not live in your land, because they will make you sin against Me; for if you serve their gods, it is certain to be a trap for you [resulting in judgment]."

— Exodus 23:24 -25, 32-33 (AMP)

God—the One True, Self-Existent God—is the only One worthy of worship.

During the great Exodus, God set Himself apart by defeating all the gods the Egyptians worshipped. God made His preeminence above all gods known to Egyptians and Israelites alike. In addition, the Israelites *saw* Him in the pillars of cloud and fire—and when they *heard* His voice, they begged Him to speak only to Moses. He showed them that He was alive and active.

The first three commandments addressed how the Israelites were to relate to God—Him alone, no graven images of other gods—and revere His name (Exod. 20:1-7). God will not compete for our affection. He will not compete for our worship or devotion. He is looking for hearts that are fully devoted to Him alone. Those are the ones He will use to accomplish His purposes. Those are the ones He will guide with His voice. Those are the ones He will shepherd.

We may not have "graven images" as they had in Egypt, but I heard a pastor once say that anything that consumes our affection and attention is a god to us. What is consuming my attention? Is there anything holding my devotion other than Him? If I think more about those things than Him, they might be gods to me.

God made it clear that He is a jealous God and there should be no other gods in our hearts. Each person must seek God on their own and choose to serve Him or serve another. Everything we do either exalts Him or exalts another. The world competes for my attention. He asks me to choose. How will I respond?

Self-Reflection: As followers and believers of God, we should intentionally ask Him to reveal anything in our lives that is competing for our affection so that we may live a life fully devoted to Him. May I choose Him daily above all others. May He alone hold my deepest affection, attention, and devotion.

Prayer: Father, forgive me where I've given my affections to the world—for the times I've chosen the things of this world over You. Capture my heart anew. You are gracious and good. Your leadership in my life is perfect, and You can be trusted. Amen.

Daily Reading: Exodus 22–24

DWELLING PLACE

And let them make Me a sanctuary, that I may dwell among them.

—Exodus 25:8 (NKJV)

The thought that God wants to dwell among and with me wrecks my heart. Why would the God of the Universe want to do that, considering who I am and how I have failed? And quietly I hear His whisper: *Because I love you, made a way for you, and it has all been forgiven.*

The Hebrew word used for dwell in this verse, *shâkan,* means the idea of lodging, residing permanently, or a place to remain or rest.

The instructions in Exodus to build Moses's Tabernacle—the tangible, physical place on Earth that the presence of God would inhabit—were precise and specific.

His instructions are still precise and specific: "If you confess with your mouth the Lord Jesus and believe in your heart that God has raised Him from the dead, you will be saved. For with the heart one believes unto righteousness, and with the mouth confession is made unto salvation. For the Scripture says, "Whoever believes on Him will not be put to shame." For there is no distinction between Jew and Greek, for the same Lord over all is rich to all who call upon Him. For whoever calls on the name of the Lord shall be saved" (Rom. 10:9 - 13 [NKJV])

His desire to dwell among us was so strong that He sent His Only Son as a sacrifice for me and you. Now, His dwelling place is inside anyone who calls upon Him, whose hearts are truly His.

Self-Reflection: He desires deep communion with us. He desires intimacy with us. He desires to dwell within us. We enlarge His dwelling place within us by reading His Word, through thanksgiving, praise, fasting, praying and interceding. May we intentionally create space for Him.

Prayer: Father, forgive me for crowding Your dwelling space in my heart with fears, worries, and things of this world. You are the only One worthy of the throne of my heart. Make your home within me. You are good. You can be trusted, and Your leadership in my life is perfect. Amen.

Daily Reading: Exodus 25–27

SWEET AROMA

. . .for a sweet aroma, an offering made by fire to the Lord. This shall be a continual burnt offering throughout your generations at the door of the tabernacle of meeting before the Lord, where I will meet you to speak with you. And there I will meet with the children of Israel, and the tabernacle shall be sanctified by My glory. . .I will dwell among the children of Israel and will be their God."

—Exodus 29:41-43, 45 (NKJV)

This verse reminds me of something the Lord spoke to me years ago: *your pain is a beautiful offering.*

I still remember kneeling at the altar during a Shady Grove worship encounter crying out about rejection from the hands of "Christians" because of my past, and as a result, thoughts like "you'll never be good enough" combined with suicidal ideations clamped down on my battered mind. I was trying to worship and said something in prayer like, "Lord! I have *nothing*! I will never be enough!" He responded with a whisper: *"Give Me your pain. Your pain is a beautiful offering."*

Mind. Blown.

Before this worship encounter, I thought worship was just "good" things. However, at the altar, He reframed what "offering" meant to me personally. He said to my heart that He wanted *everything*. My brokenness, pain, rejection, anger, et cetera. He wanted every part of it—especially the ugly stuff.

This passage is a beautiful reminder that my brokenness is like the burnt offering—a pleasing aroma to Him. That moment at the altar reframed my view of brokenness. I believe the things that burn me—the brokenness both past and present that sears my heart—are all part of Him purifying me to be more like Him.

Self-Reflection: More of Him. Less of me. No matter the cost. No matter how hot. I just want to be a pleasing aroma to Him.

Prayer: Father—Give me grace and strength to trust you. You are good. You can be trusted, and Your leadership in my life is perfect. Amen.

Daily reading: Exodus 28–29

BE THE BUFFALO

*Now when the people saw that Moses delayed coming down from the
mountain, they gathered together before Aaron and said to him, "Come,
make us a god who will go before us; as for this Moses, the man who
brought us up from the land of Egypt, we do not know what has become
of him." So Aaron replied to them, "Take off the gold rings that are in the
ears of your wives, your sons and daughters, and bring them to me." So all
the people took off the gold rings that were in their ears and brought them
to Aaron. And he took the gold from their hands, and fashioned it with an
engraving tool and made it into a molten calf; and they said, "This is your
god, O Israel, who brought you up from the land of Egypt." Now when
Aaron saw the molten calf, he built an altar before it; and Aaron made a
proclamation, and said, "Tomorrow shall be a feast to the Lord!"*

—Exodus 32:1-5 (AMP)

There is so much happening in Exodus 32, and while I want
to blame it all on the impatience of the Israelites, I was struck
instead by Aaron's response to their complaint.

Moses delayed. He was gone for 40 days. We have no idea
how long it had been from the time of the plagues until this
point in time, but it was at the beginning of what would become
a 40-year journey. And, in just 40 days, they turned from "Yes
Lord! We will do what you say!!" (Exodus 24:3) to worship a

golden calf. Just *40* days!

In just 40 days of waiting, they grew impatient and asked Aaron to make them a god, and Aaron said *yes*! How did they make the jump so quickly?

Aaron, who was an intricate part of and had a front-row seat to the many miracles God performed in Egypt, Aaron, who witnessed everything *firsthand*, gave up and gave in when the people complained instead of reminding them what God had done.

Aaron's response mattered. Aaron asked for their gold. Aaron fashioned the calf. Aaron built an altar. Aaron proclaimed the feast, and the people worshipped—a calf of all things—with great abandonment, so much in fact that Joshua thought the sound he heard was the sound of war in the camp. (Exod. 32:17–18). I ponder Aaron's response and wonder how things might have been different if he had responded differently and led the people through their fear instead of giving in.

Of course, we will never know how things might have been different as it was all a part of God's plan in the end, but as a leader, there is a message here for me: leadership matters. Whether I lead at home or at the office, how I respond to my family and team during moments of fear and crisis *does* make a difference. I have a choice in how I will respond to others in moments of crisis and pain.

At the Global Leadership Summit in 2021, I adopted a new motto after listening to Best-Selling Author Shola Richards: Be the buffalo. He explained that one of the critical differences between cows and buffalo is how they respond to storms: one runs away from it, and the other turns into it. Cows run in the same direction of a storm and tire quickly. But the buffalo turns *into* a storm and plods forward. As a result, buffalo come through the storm much faster. Buffalo are solid and resilient, and their response to storms is a lesson to me as a leader. In difficulty, I want to "Be the buffalo." Sometimes, I stand firm. Sometimes, the storm knocks me over, but I get up and keep plodding forward.

Self-Reflection: As a leader, I want to inspire my family and others to stand as firmly in the storms as they have in the sunshine. I want to encourage them to dig deeper and hold on longer. I do not want to give up too soon and "worship a calf"—I want to hold on and stand firm, knowing that God is good, He can be trusted, and His leadership is perfect. Whatever we are facing—good or bad—may He find us standing strong, waiting for Him to come. He might be closer than we think.

Prayer: Father, I love You. Thank You for constantly pursuing and teaching me. Help me to stand firm. Amen.

Daily reading: Exodus 30–32

UNIQUELY RADIANT

When Moses came down from Mount Sinai with the two tablets of the Testimony in his hand, he did not know that the skin of his face was shining [with a unique radiance] because he had been speaking with God.

—Exodus 34:29 (AMP)

Moses endured another forty days and forty nights without bread or water in the presence of God, and it visibly changed his appearance! One would think he would be pale, with a sunken face after not eating for so long, but he wasn't! His face glowed! And it kept glowing every time He met with God!

Initially the Israelites were afraid to approach Moses but quickly returned when he spoke to them (v. 30–31), and each time Moses met with God, Moses continued to bear a unique radiance. Interestingly, the change in Moses's appearance came at this point. Moses met with God many times before. Moses encountered Him in the burning bush, heard His voice through the plagues, and spent 40 days with God. Then, the crisis of the calf, and another 40 days. It was in this second 40-day period that Moses was visibly transformed. Why not the others? I think it was because God revealed His glory and nature to Moses and physically came near him: "Then the Lord passed by in front of him, and proclaimed, 'The Lord, the Lord God, compassionate and gracious, slow to anger, and abounding in lovingkindness and truth (faithfulness); keeping mercy and lovingkindness for thousands, forgiving iniquity and transgression and sin; but He will by no means leave the guilty unpunished, visiting (avenging) the iniquity (sin, guilt) of the fathers upon the children and the grandchildren to the third and fourth generations [that is, calling the children to account for the sins of their fathers].' Moses bowed to the earth immediately and worshiped [the Lord]" (Exod. 34:6-8 [AMP])

The presence of God is transformative, and the more times we encounter Him, and the more time we spend in the presence of God, the more He transforms us into His image. And the transformation should be obvious to those around us. My countenance and life should carry a unique radiance that causes others to see Him clearly in and through me.

Self-Reflection: Each one has their own journey with Him. He alone is the only One with the power to transform us and make us truly radiant. May we be encouraged by the truth that His presence goes with us along the way.

Prayer: Father, thank You for pursuing me. Transform my heart and life into Your image. Make me a mirror of Your nature and character to those around me. You are good. You can be trusted, and Your leadership in my life is perfect. Amen.

Daily Reading: Exodus 33–35

STIRRED UP

"So Bezalel and Oholiab are to work, along with every wise-hearted
man in whom Adonai has placed insight and understanding to know
how to perform all the labor for the service of the Sanctuary, according to
everything Adonai has commanded." Then Moses called Bezalel, Oholiab
and all the wise-hearted men in whose minds Adonai had set wisdom,
along with everyone whose heart stirred him up to come do the work.

—Exodus 36:1-2 (TLV)

God is the giver of talents and abilities. He puts wisdom, ideas, and creativity in our hearts. As a mom and leader, part of my responsibility is to be attentive and listen for the things stirring in my son's and daughter's hearts, then help them shepherd and cultivate those gifts. It is also my responsibility to look within at what He has put in my own heart to the things He is stirring in me.

In this verse, the Hebrew word for the phrase "stirred him up" is *nâsâ'*, and in this passage, it carries the meaning "of heart-lifting one *up*."

The imagery is pretty accurate: your heart lifting you up. I know the feeling of my heart being stirred up. I still remember the day God called me to serve my mentor, Pastor Olen. I was listening to him preach at a worship seminar when my heart felt like it was being pulled out of my chest. I knew immediately I was called to serve him and was honored to do so for twelve years. Over the years, I have felt other stirrings. Once, I felt led to take an exit and immediately noticed a homeless man with a sign. He had long blond hair and held a sign that said Myrtle Beach. While waiting for the light to turn, I heard a whisper in my heart to send the prodigal home, and stirred to obey, I did. Throughout my walk with God, I have felt other promptings and stirrings to serve, to go, or to write. For years, I was labeled as "too emotional," yet I wonder how much of that "emotion" was a stirring in my spirit, my heart lifting me up, that I simply did not understand or recognize yet.

Self-Reflection: When our heart is all stirred up, it is something to pay attention to. We may not be called to build Moses's Tabernacle, but He could be calling us to build something else for His glory, and when our hearts are lifted to Him, there's a sense of fulfillment and joy that cannot be described.

Prayer: Father, help me to identify the stirrings when they come —to see what You have put in my heart. Give me ears to hear Your voice and eyes to see Your hand. I want to build Your kingdom. Stir me up for what stirs You. You are good. You can be trusted, and Your leadership in my life is perfect. Amen.

Daily Reading: Exodus 36–38

QUALIFIED

*You shall put the holy garments on Aaron and anoint him and consecrate
him, that he may serve as a priest to Me.*

—Exodus 40:13 (AMP)

Reading this passage, I was struck by the incredible detail
that went into the Tabernacle. Each article and garment were
intricately designed, and when it was all said and done, the
guy who made the golden calf and led the Israelites in their
worship of a false god was consecrated, set aside, and made a
priest unto God!

His past transgression forgiven, Aaron was given holy garments,
anointed, and consecrated.

When I was two, I had bacterial spinal meningitis, and the
doctors did not think I would make it. One told my parents that
I would never amount to anything, and another told my mom
to go home and prepare for my funeral. But God! He had a plan
for me that would not and could not be thwarted by disease,
divorce, depression, or abuse. His plans for me and His call on
me are irrevocable.

No matter what we have done, God still wants to use us. No matter how we have failed, He makes a way for us. When the world calls us disqualified, He promotes us. It's a pretty humbling thought.

Self-Reflection: When we say yes to God, He clothes us in priestly garments, He anoints us, and He consecrates us through His Son. The doubts and insecurities whispering in our ears are nothing more than a web of lies. We can choose to believe the lies, or we can choose to believe the truth that because of Him, we are qualified. I choose Truth.

Prayer: Father—thank You for forgiving me. Thank You for rescuing me from abuse and depression. Thank You for restoring and healing me. You are good. You can be trusted, and Your leadership in my life is perfect. Amen.

Daily Reading: Exodus 39–40

SEASONED WITH SALT

And every offering of your grain offering you shall season with salt; you shall not allow the salt of the covenant of your God to be lacking from your grain offering. With all your offerings you shall offer salt.

—Leviticus 2:13 (NKJV)

Salt is a simple seasoning everyone has in their home and whose properties do not change. Most of us learned that trick in science— pour salt in boiling water, and when the water evaporates, salt crystals remain. So fascinating!

From what I could tell with a quick word search, salt is mentioned approximately forty times in the Bible. It's been around a long time! And in this passage, it is mentioned as part of an offering.

Salt is used for many things in our daily lives, but two uses stand out to me as I read this passage: for seasoning and for preserving. First, salt is a seasoning. We all know when something is too salty or not salty enough, and just like I know whether a dish has enough salt or too much, I must listen to the Spirit to know when to sprinkle salt and when I've sprinkled enough. I do not want to be "extra" and push people away like a dish that cannot be eaten because it is too salty. Rather, I believe my life and daily interactions should leave people craving Him, not pushing Him away. I am often quite thirsty after I eat salty food—like pizza or Chinese. Likewise, my life should leave others thirsty for Him. Second, salt is a preservative. Salt helps dehydrate foods so they last longer. Some foods, such as capers and anchovies, come packed in salt. Salt also reduces the growth of bacteria. The Bible tells Believers to be the "salt of the earth." As Believers, we are to preserve God's Word and His ways in the earth, and our lives of faith should bring seasoning to those around us (Matt. 5:13).

The "salt of the covenant" or "covenant of salt" appears three times in the Bible: Leviticus 2:13, 2 Chronicles 13:5, and Numbers 18:19. A "salt covenant" seems to imply that the covenant is everlasting, perpetual, and unchanging.

On Shabbat in our home, we salt the bread for three reasons: to remind us of His everlasting covenant with the Jewish people and with those who call upon His Son for salvation, to remind us to be salt and light to a decaying world, and to remember the salty tears of the Israelites during slavery as a reminder to ourselves that our tears will not last forever.

Self-Reflection: His promises to us are unchanging. He will keep His Word, and He will preserve our lives. He is not a man that would lie. He is good, and He can be trusted.

Prayer: Father, thank You for making a way for me. Thank You for grace. Make my life light and salt for You. Shine through me. May others "taste" You when they meet me. Your leadership in my life is perfect, and I trust You. Amen.

Daily Reading: Leviticus 1–4

ALWAYS BURNING

Then the Lord spoke to Moses, saying, "Command Aaron and his sons,
saying, 'This is the law of the burnt offering: The burnt offering shall be on
the hearth upon the altar all night until morning, and the fire of the altar
shall be kept burning on it. And the priest shall put on his linen garment,
and his linen trousers he shall put on his body, and take up the ashes of
the burnt offering which the fire has consumed on the altar, and he shall
put them beside the altar. Then he shall take off his garments, put on other
garments, and carry the ashes outside the camp to a clean place. And the
fire on the altar shall be kept burning on it; it shall not be put out. And
the priest shall burn wood on it every morning, and lay the burnt offering
in order on it; and he shall burn on it the fat of the peace offerings. A fire
shall always be burning on the altar; it shall never go out."

—Leviticus 6:8-13 (NKJV)

Burnt offerings are believed to be the oldest and most common
offerings in the Bible. Noah offered burnt offerings in Genesis
8:20, and God ordered Abraham to offer his son as a burnt
offering in Genesis 22. While many offerings are mentioned
in Leviticus, a "burnt offering" was significant because it was
the only offering completely consumed by fire, minus only the
hide of the animal, and the burnt offering symbolized a desire to
renew and restore a relationship with God. The Hebrew word for

"burnt offering," *'ôlâ*, means to step up or ascend, as on stairs, or to go up in smoke—literally to burn completely.

God commanded that this type of offering burn continually and not be allowed to "go out." The Hebrew word used for that phrase is *kâbâh*, meaning to be quenched or to be extinguished. God desires a continual "burning" before Him—that our hearts "go up before Him" day and night. It is costly, and it requires sacrifice, but it is what He desires—relationship, not acquaintanceship.

I find the part about the priest removing the ashes from the altar interesting. When we lived in the country, we burned all paper-type trash. It smelled good and was nice to look at, but it was messy, and if you stood near the burn barrel, you would soon have ash on you. Additionally, the ash that collected in the bottom of the barrel eventually had to be cleaned out to make room for the fire to keep burning. I once offered to help my dad clean the ash out of the barrel, but he replied that it was a "one-person job" because the person cleaning the barrel would get ash all over them. As I meditate anew on this passage, God whispers these words to my heart: *"It is a One-person job, Marci."*

God provided the One sacrifice that restores my relationship to Him. He is the One High Priest who receives and cleans up the ashes of my burnt offering. Offerings are costly—He gave His Only Son.

The "wood on the fire" is the fuel. When I spend time praising and thanking Him, I bring wood for the fire. When I prioritize His presence over things that do not please Him, I bring more wood for the fire. When I obey His voice, even when it is costly, or when I go wherever He sends me, I bring more wood for the fire. When I surrender my brokenness and offer forgiveness, I bring more wood for the fire. The wood may be costly, but it fuels the fire of my relationship with Him.

And the ashes? He carries them to a clean place outside the camp, and the significance is obvious. One Person. One Priest. He alone cleans up my mess. He alone carries the ashes of my life—the brokenness and the offerings—to a clean place. He makes the offering of my life holy through His Son.

Self-Reflection: I'm messy—but He is OK with that. He is the only One worthy of all I have to give and the only One who can clean up the ashes of my life so there is room for the fire to keep burning.

Prayer: Father, More of You. Less of me. Clean out the ashes that I might burn continually for You alone. You are good. You can be trusted, and Your leadership in my life is perfect. Amen.

Daily Reading: Leviticus 5–7

REGARD HIM

And Moses said to Aaron, "This is what the Lord spoke, saying: 'By those who come near Me I must be regarded as holy; And before all the people I must be glorified.'" So Aaron held his peace.

—Leviticus 10:3 (NKJV)

Regard—from the Middle and Old English. To guard or to look upon. The Hebrew word used in this phrase is qāḏaš, to be treated as sacred.

The first time I held my son and my daughter felt like a sacred moment. As I held them, I remember being overcome by the thought that God had formed them by His own hand. I remember how carefully I held them, fully supporting their neck and head, cradling and protecting them. In those early hours and days, I just wanted to hold them and be close to them. The Lord brought this picture to mind and spoke to my heart that I should approach Him the same way. I should cherish and guard His presence, regarding Him alone as sacred. I must recognize how precious He is and how cherished His presence really is. Always holding an awareness of Him and His presence within me and clinging closely to Him. He alone is truly sacred. His presence is precious and cherished, and it should be guarded and regarded above *all* things in my life.

I wonder how often I enter His presence distracted and unaware, taking for granted that I am approaching *the One* True *Holy* God of the Universe—the Self-Existent One, Jehovah. God. The One who's name is considered too holy to write fully, so the Jewish people use a dash to show honor to Him. His presence alone is what is truly sacred.

I always say I value my alone time and Shabbat, but do I value time with Him as much? Do I protect and cherish His presence as much as I cherish and protect my Friday schedule at work? Not always. I dare say I take His presence for granted far too often.

Self-Reflection: Sometimes, I relegate God to a certain time in my day or week. Sometimes, I get so busy and distracted that I forget He is *inside me*. He is sacred; therefore, it is time to act like it and start guarding, regarding, looking upon, and treating Him as such again.

Prayer: Father, forgive me for being flippant about Your presence and taking You for granted. Capture my heart again. You are the Only One worthy. I look to You alone and place You in the highest place in my life. You are good. Your leadership in my life is perfect, and You can be trusted. Amen.

Daily Reading: Leviticus 8–10

MAKE A DISTINCTION

For I am Adonai who brought you up out of the land of Egypt, to be your God. Therefore, you should be holy, for I am holy. This is the Torah of the animal, the bird, every living creature that moves in the waters, and every creature that creeps on the earth, to make a distinction between the unclean and the clean, and between the living thing that may be eaten and the living thing that may not be eaten.

—Leviticus 11:45-47 (TLV)

Translations are interesting to me. It took ten English words to translate one Hebrew word in the passage above. The *one* Hebrew word for the entire phrase above, "to make a distinction between the clean and the unclean," is *bâdal*, more specifically this means to make a distinction between the holy and profane.

While this verse specifically talks about food and clean versus unclean animals, I think the principle applies to everything: what we eat or drink, what we watch or do not watch, what we read or do not read, et cetera. As I told my children from when they were a very young age, everything we do or say and everything we watch or listen to either honors God or dishonors Him. There's no gray area in holiness.

Years ago, I asked a young missionary friend who was home on sabbatical with her parents if she was happy to be back in the States. She immediately answered no. I was shocked! When I asked her to explain, she said it was easier to be a Christian in their country because there was a clear distinction between believers and nonbelievers. Overseas, people who had a relationship with God lived and acted differently and it was obvious. She could easily identify Christians overseas, while in America, she found people too compromised and living in the gray area. She said she hated the hypocrisy in American Christians. Her story marked me. She had a valid point.

Since I am a follower of and believer in God, there should be an obvious, clear distinction in my life. When someone looks at my life or interacts with me, am I mirroring, reflecting, and sounding like the world, or am I mirroring, reflecting, and sounding like the Kingdom of God? Sadly, I sometimes feel like my spiritual senses have become dull rather than distinct.

Self-Reflection: My choices matter—what I put in will flow out. It's a simple principle. More of Him. Less of me. When there's more of Him in me, others will see more of Him. May my life and my words *bâdal*, clearly distinguishing between the holy and the profane.

Prayer: Father, thank You for grace and forgiveness. Thank You for Your conviction. Turn my heart to You alone. Make my life a distinction for Your glory. You are good. You can be trusted, and Your leadership in my life is perfect. Amen.

Daily Reading: Leviticus 11–13

AS I AM

Then the priest who makes him clean shall present the man who is to be made clean, and those things, before the Lord, at the door of the tabernacle of meeting. . . . The rest of the oil that is in the priest's hand he shall put on the head of him who is to be cleansed. So the priest shall make atonement for him before the Lord.

—Leviticus 14:11, 18 (NKJV)

Leviticus is full of detailed instructions regarding offerings and being made clean. There were stringent guidelines to the offerings brought into the Tabernacle—what, when, and how often they were to be brought—but in each case, only one person presented the offering to God—the priest. For years, I had a picture of dropping off the offering at the Tabernacle entrance and then walking away. That was not the case!

The verses above are about one particular type of offering for one particular type of man: a healed leper. Picture this—a leper who was previously outside of the camp, who walked around proclaiming he was unclean while tearing his clothes (Lev. 13:45–46), suddenly found himself with clean skin standing with the priest at the door of the tabernacle of meeting. After the offerings were made and rituals done, the priest's last act was to anoint the head of the leper with oil, declaring the leaper clean and healed.

What a picture of restoration!

This man once rejected and outcast because of his condition, who was required to announce his disease to everyone, endured physical pain and emotional isolation all alone. People surely saw him *as* the disease. His disease became his identity.

Yet, in the verses between the dots above, the priest poured oil into his own hand and used it to anoint the healed leper's right ear, right thumb, and right toe, and the rest of the oil was placed on his head.

God made a way for a man once rejected and outcast to be restored, forgiven, and truly healed.

Maybe the significance of anointing his thumb with oil was to restore his sense of purpose—after all, we work with our hands, and most of us find purpose there. Maybe the significance of anointing his ear with oil was to restore his thoughts—after all, so much of what we think about ourselves is just a recording of what someone has spoken over us, including our own voice. Maybe the significance of anointing his big toe with oil was to restore his way—to set him on a new path and allow him to walk whole. And maybe, just maybe, placing the hand with the remaining oil on his head was a priestly blessing—a welcoming home, an imparting of peace and of spiritual and emotional wholeness.

Self-Reflection: He offers no less to me and you. No matter what happened in our past, He is our present and future. Our identity is now found in Him alone.

Prayer: Father, thank You for healing and restoring me. I am forever grateful. You are good to me. Your leadership in my life is perfect, and You can be trusted. Amen.

Daily Reading: Leviticus 14–15

TWO GOATS

Aaron shall cast lots for the two goats—one lot for the Lord, the other lot for the scapegoat...Then Aaron shall lay both of his hands on the head of the live goat, and confess over it all the wickedness of the sons of Israel and all their transgressions in regard to all their sins; and he shall lay them on the head of the goat [the scapegoat, the sin-bearer], and send it away into the wilderness by the hand of a man who is prepared [for the task]. The goat shall carry on itself all their (the Israelites) wickedness, carrying them to a solitary (infertile) land; and he shall release the goat in the wilderness.

—Leviticus 16:8, 21-22 (AMP)

Chapter 16 might be my favorite one in Leviticus because it speaks of the Day of Atonement—the *one* day when the high priest could enter the Holy of Holies. So much symbolism is found here—like hidden gems waiting to be discovered! As I was rereading and meditating on it, the two goats held particular meaning for me.

The first goat killed, its blood a sacrifice for sins, and the second, the precious scapegoat, the one who symbolically carried the sin out of the camp.

It is interesting to me that the high priest would place his hands on the head of the scapegoat, confess the wickedness over it, then release it to be led to the solitary place.

As believers, we know that Yeshua was our scapegoat. Once and for all, He removed the penalty of sin. He provided the blood sacrifice required. Yet far too often in my life, the little scapegoat wanders back into my "camp," carrying the guilt, the shame, the memories, and the reminders of my past long forgiven.

Could the first goat represent grace and the second goat represent mercy? After all, it is by grace that I have been forgiven, and it is because of mercy that I no longer carry shame and guilt from my past.

The Day of Atonement observed once a year must have been a day of radical encounter with God. Just imagine it: one day dedicated solely to seeking out sin and wickedness, both hidden and known sins, offering sacrifices, burning incense, and encountering His forgiveness, the scapegoat, the reminder that sin, shame, and guilt "left the camp," not to return.

I do not take one day out of the year to focus on the sin in my life—to intentionally seek Him to discover what areas of my life do not glorify Him—but maybe I should. My heart is convicted that I often take grace for granted. Am I quick to respond to His conviction to repent and seek forgiveness? Am I quick to repent and ask forgiveness for wronging my husband or children with words or actions? Do I extend forgiveness when I've been broken? Do I live and love like one forgiven? Sin is serious business—do I approach it as such?

Self-Reflection: Sin separates me from the Almighty God! At all costs, I should have a fiery resolve and intolerance of sin in my life. More of Him, less of me—all because the Scapegoat found a way into my heart twenty-four years ago.

Prayer: Father, more of You, less of me because You alone are worthy. Purify my heart, God. Bring to mind anything I am doing or saying, reading or watching, that is a sin or is opening the door to it. You are good. Your leadership in my life is perfect, and You can be trusted. Amen.

Daily Reading: Leviticus 16–18

OFFERED FREELY

And if you offer a sacrifice of a peace offering to the Lord, you shall offer it of your own free will.

—Leviticus 19:5 (NKJV)

This verse leaped off the page at me. *If* you offer a "sacrifice of peace offering," it must be of your own free will. *If* you offer it, not when you offer it, but if you offer it, do it willingly.

The Hebrew word for peace offering is šelem, which means a voluntary sacrifice in thanks and a sacrifice showing an alliance for friendship, specifically friendship between God and man.

Such a powerful thought! When I bring a *šelem*, pronounced sheh'-lem, freely and willingly from my heart, it is a type of holy offering to Him and an expression of my friendship with Him.

Robert Emmons, leading scientific researcher and expert on the science of gratitude, defines gratitude as "an affirmation of goodness. We affirm that there are good things in the world, gifts and benefits we've received." True gratitude is far more than the rote or conditioned "thank you" when someone holds the door for us or helps us with something. It is a deep awareness and recognition of goodness bestowed upon us.

The Greater Good Science Center, a part of UC Berkeley, has a deep repository of the proven benefits of a "gratitude practice." Research studies by non-Christian scientists have identified many physical benefits of a gratitude practice. One study cited improvements such as an increase in brain activity in the decision center of the brain and a significant decrease in both blood pressure and heart rate when participants incorporated a regular practice of gratitude into their daily routine for just three months. If intentionally giving thanks and expressing gratitude is good for our physical bodies, imagine how a peace offering brought before *the* King of the Universe benefits our spirit!

When expressing gratitude depends on how I "feel" or what I'm experiencing, it can seem like a sacrifice. Sometimes it's hard to dig up gratitude when I feel buried. But, ironically, gratitude is the light that will lead me out of the darkness that surrounds me and lighten the heaviness I feel.

When šelem becomes a lifestyle, when I intentionally affirm His goodness to me, I am transformed.

Self-Reflection: He won't force me to come. He doesn't demand it of me. He simply desires me. He is just that good.

Prayer: Father, transform my heart. Your goodness undoes me. You've healed me and redeemed me. You've restored me and given me Your favor. You made a way and gave Your Son for me just because You love me. You are truly good. Your leadership in my life is perfect, and I fully trust You. Amen.

Daily Reading: Leviticus 19–21

FEASTS FOREVER

Speak to the children of Israel, and say to them: "The feasts of the Lord, which you shall proclaim to be holy convocations, these are My feasts... that your generations may know that I made the children of Israel dwell in booths when I brought them out of the land of Egypt: I am the Lord your God." So Moses declared to the children of Israel the feasts of the Lord.

—Leviticus 23:2, 43-44 (NKJV)

In Leviticus 23, God proclaimed that the Israelites were to observe a total of eight feasts—one weekly and seven annually: Shabbat, Passover, Unleavened Bread, First Fruits, Pentecost, Trumpets, Atonement, and Tabernacles.

God called each observance a Holy Convocation. They were to gather together at seven set times a year and once weekly, united around one purpose: to know and remember that He alone was the Lord, their God.

People have often asked us why we observe Jewish customs and not traditional church ones. No, we are not Jewish, but we deeply love the Jewish people and feel passionately about their God. We firmly believe the Biblical mandate that they are His chosen people.

Our hearts were fully awakened to the Jewish feasts through a combination of our five-year-old son, personal experience, and our homeschool curriculum. Randal asked us why we didn't observe the Sabbath after watching a movie about the Ten Commandments, and I didn't have a good answer. We were fortunate to be mentored by a couple who taught us the significance of the biblical feasts and how we could begin by incorporating the Sabbath.

The homeschool curriculum we used a few years later opened our eyes to the rest of the feasts and thus began our journey of discovery and awakening. The intentional act of honoring God through observing His feasts transformed our hearts and our family.

We found that all of the feasts and observances had one common goal: to remember and recount the goodness and provision of God. Additionally, each observance aligned with a conviction rooted deep in our hearts that one generation shall tell the next generation of the mighty deeds of God so that they would not be stubborn and stiff-necked.

For us personally, the biblical feasts held more significance than traditional church holidays and gave us a path to teach biblical principles to our children in an intentional way while pointing them to Jesus.

Self-Reflection: As Christian parents and leaders, it is our duty to teach our children and those looking to us about God and His ways—not just one day a week, but every day. We should intentionally share His truth through word, deed, and action. The feasts are just a tool we use to do that. May our lives be a reflection of Him in all things.

Prayer: Father, thank You for giving us appointed times to reflect and recount Your goodness. Thank You for the mentors You placed in our lives to teach us. Thank You for making a way for me to participate. I pray for the peace of Israel and for the Jewish people. You are good, Lord. Your leadership in my life is perfect, and I trust You. Amen.

Daily Reading: Leviticus 22–23

A Purposeful Pause

They put him in custody until the will and command of the Lord might be made clear to them.

—Leviticus 24:12 (AMP)

When Randal and Alathia were toddlers and they did something I did not know how to respond to, I often sent them to their room so I could pray and ask the Holy Spirit what to do. And after I prayed, I would take a deep breath and wait. More often than not, I would hear a response for the moment or situation I faced.

While the situation in the verse above doesn't fit the circumstances, the principle does: when you do not know what to do, wait until the will and voice of the Lord is clear.

The Hebrew word used for the phrase "in custody" is *mišmār* and means a guardhouse or to stand guard. Interestingly, the same word is used in Proverbs 4:23 to describe how we are to "guard" our hearts: "Watch over your heart with all diligence, for from it flow the springs of life."

In other words, we should stand guard at the gates of our heart to protect what goes into and out of it.

When I put my kids in this type of "time-out," for lack of a better term, I did so to protect their hearts and mine. I was setting up a guard.

Scientists have discovered that we make approximately 35,000 decisions a day. Of those, roughly 20 percent are conscious and 80 percent are subconscious. Additionally, most decisions are made within 5 to 7 *seconds*. That means we make approximately 25,000 decisions a day from a subconscious state where our emotions, memories, and experiences—both good and bad—are stored. Essentially, we are making most of our decisions, and thereby formulating most of our responses, based on the past.

Self-Reflection: If we can take a purposeful pause and wait for God to speak to us, we can make decisions based on Truth and we can respond like He would respond—with intention and with love.

Prayer: Father, help me love like You love. Give me Your grace. Redeem my mind, emotions, and memories so that I glorify and honor you in all things. You are good. Your leadership in my life is perfect, and You can be trusted. Amen.

Daily Reading: Leviticus 24–25

A PEACEFUL PORTION

If you walk in My statutes and keep My commandments and [obediently]
do them, then I will give you rain in its season, and the land will yield her
produce and the trees of the field bear their fruit. . .I will also grant peace
in the land, so that you may lie down and there will be no one to make
you afraid. . . .For I will turn toward you [with favor and regard] and
make you fruitful and multiply you, and I will establish and confirm My
covenant with you.

—Leviticus 26:3-4,6,9 (AMP)

I love this chapter! After rereading it a few times, a thought came to me: the measure of peace I experience is proportionate to my level of obedience. He promises me a peaceful portion *if* I heed His voice and walk in His ways.

The word used in this verse for peace is *shâlôm*, pronounced shaw-lome—the same word used in the sabbath greeting "Shabbat shalom." In addition to peace, the word means a place of safety, good health, and wholeness.

Self-Reflection: True peace is found in a relationship with God. When we disobey Him, we open doors in our hearts and minds through which peace escapes. Repentance closes the door, and His presence restores the peace.

Prayer: Father, show me where I have open doors. Forgive me for doubt and fear. Heal my painful memories and give me Your peace. You are good. Your leadership in my life is perfect, and You can be trusted. Amen.

Daily Reading: Leviticus 26–27

PROFESSIONAL MOVERS

But appoint the Levites over the tabernacle (sanctuary) of the Testimony, and over all its furnishings and all things that belong to it. They shall carry the tabernacle [when traveling] and all its furnishings, and they shall take care of it and camp around it.... The Levites shall be in charge of the tabernacle of the Testimony.

—Numbers 1:50, 53 (AMP)

Moving is something I easily relate to. We are practically pros! We have done it alone, used friends and family to help, and used professional movers—and learned that hiring professionals is worth it, especially for the big stuff.

The Tabernacle was large and ornate. There were many components made of solid gold—one being the Mercy Seat where the physical presence of God dwelt in the Tent of Meeting.

The Levites were professional movers of the presence of God. They were charged with packing the articles, carrying them, then setting them up again. Essentially, the Levites were protectors of the presence of God.

As believers, we are modern-day Levites. We are "professional movers" of God's presence. We carry His presence inside of us wherever we go, and wherever we stop to "set up camp," His presence is established. At work, at home, in the store, at church, at the gym—anywhere we go, we carry His presence.

Self-Reflection: It is a good reminder that I am a mover of His presence. He is always with me because the Holy Spirit dwells within me, and wherever I go, I am never alone. He's there to give me peace and wisdom. He's there to protect me. He provides for and cares for me. I may not have to carry the physically heavy furnishings of the Tabernacle, but His presence is weighty and must be handled carefully. May I be ever mindful of the Presence I carry within me.

Prayer: Father, thank You for dwelling in me! It's humbling that You would choose *me* as a dwelling place! Thank You! May I live and love worthy of You. You are good. Your leadership in my life is perfect, and You can be trusted. Amen.

Daily Reading: Numbers 1–2

A CHILD TENDED HIM

According to the number of all the males, from a month old and above,
there were eight thousand, six hundred keeping charge of the sanctuary.
The families of the children of Kohath were to camp on the south side of
the tabernacle...Their duty included the ark, the table, the lampstand, the
altars, the utensils of the sanctuary with which they ministered, the screen,
and all the work relating to them.

—Numbers 3:28-29, 31 (NKJV)

What a humbling truth that resonates with something I have felt strongly about for years—children have a place in the sanctuary!

I read *Parenting from the Pew* when we lived in Tyler. The author, a pastor's wife, explained how they included their children in the church service from infancy. There were many good ideas that resonated with me. The best place for children in church is in the pew, alongside their parents. They belong there as much as—if not more than—anyone!

Several years ago I heard a powerful message at Shady Grove by Lou Engle. One of the points of his sermon was the idea that an abortion mentality was rampant in the church and among Christians. He explained that an abortion mentality viewed children as both inconvenient and a burden. It might sound something like, "I cannot be bothered to work in the nursery because I do not like snotty noses or do not want to miss the sermon." But a life mentality says children are a gift and a blessing! He theorized that a church that turned away nursery volunteers was a church that was alive and in revival. In other words, *life* mentality welcomes revival. We cannot say we truly support life if we want nothing to do with children.

Research shows that 80 to 90 percent of children raised in church stop attending once they graduate high school. The number is staggering and concerning. Could the numbers be high because "church" is not personal do them? Could it be because they do not know how to serve in "big" church? After all, "big" church is a much different experience! Gone are the entertainment, fun, and games.

God's design was for children—one month and up—to be a part of sanctuary ministry. Yes, they need to be trained to be quiet and shown how to participate. Yes, they may get loud. Yes, it is exhausting at times. Yes, it would be nice to "have a break." Yet if we truly desire to raise children who passionately pursue God, we must train them intentionally. One hour a week isn't enough. They will learn to worship by watching us. They will learn to love His presence by participating in worship. They will learn the value of community and where they belong by being a part of the body.

Self-Reflection: Yeshua said to let the little children come to him. Children belong. It's that simple.

Prayer: Father, thank You for Your grace and for churches that have embraced our children over the years. Thank You for House of Grace putting wings to Alathia's dream and for our dear friends Brent, Larry, and Christina, who championed Randal as a young worship leader. Thank you for youth pastors like Ben and Oana who model a spirit-filled life. There are so many dear ones who have opened their hearts to our children, teaching them to serve You. I am grateful! You are good. Your leadership in my life is perfect, and You can be trusted. Amen.

Daily Reading: Numbers 3–4

THE

AARONIC BENEDICTION

Then the Lord spoke to Moses, saying, "Speak to Aaron and his sons, saying, 'This is the way you shall bless the Israelites. Say to them: The Lord bless you, and keep you [protect you, sustain you, and guard you]; The Lord make His face shine upon you [with favor], And be gracious to you [surrounding you with lovingkindness]; The Lord lift up His countenance (face) upon you [with divine approval], And give you peace [a tranquil heart and life].' So Aaron and his sons shall put My name upon the children of Israel, and I will bless them."

—Numbers 6:22-27 (AMP)

One of my most cherished memories is the voice of Pastor Olen singing the Aaronic Blessing at the conclusion of almost every service at Shady Grove. If I close my eyes, I can hear him in my mind and a feeling of peace falls over me like a warm blanket on an icy Texas day. Also referred to as the Priestly Blessing or the Aaronic Benediction, the words infuse the receiver with peace, hope, and strength. It is regularly sung or quoted at the end of religious services among many faiths—Catholic, Lutheran, Protestant, and Jewish—and refocuses the listener on the power of God to sustain, guide, and provide.

A benediction, by definition, is the utterance or bestowing of a blessing, especially at the end of a religious service; it is a devout or formal invocation of blessedness.

Many scholars consider the Aaronic Benediction or Priestly Blessing to be the highest form of blessing because it comes from God Himself. He instructed Aaron through Moses on exactly what to say. Additionally, the Priestly Blessing is often accompanied by a specific hand shape symbolizing Shaddai, a Hebrew name of God. Some rabbinic teachings explain that the hand shape symbolizes a lattice or window through which the Divine Presence of God shines onto the heads of those receiving it. Others teach that it is customary not to look directly at the hands of the person speaking the blessing because the words and the shape of God's name on the hands are too holy to behold, so holy that the one pronouncing the blessing will often cover their heads entirely, leaving only their hands visible.

However it is spoken or sung, whether you see the hands or you look away, the Priestly Blessing or Aaronic Benediction is powerful because the words uttered are the very words of God spoken from Him, through His priest, to and over us, His people.

Self-Reflection: Fortunately, we do not have to wait for a service or someone else to speak it to receive it. The Aaronic Benediction is still His utterance of blessing over you and me. May I have the courage to impart the power and gift of this blessing to another.

Prayer: Father, thank You for Your words of hope and blessing. Thank You for words that sustain. Guide me and use me. You are good. Your leadership in my life is perfect, and You can be trusted. Amen.

Daily Reading: Numbers 5–6

LEADERS SACRIFICE

The leaders offered the dedication sacrifices for the altar on the day that it
was anointed; and they offered their sacrifice before the altar.

—Numbers 7:10 (AMP)

The word "leader," used first in the fourteenth century to describe
a person in charge, comes from the Old English word *lædan*—
meaning to go before as a guide.

Leader. A person who guides.

I love that image—walking ahead to show the way; and
sometimes forging a new path requires cutting down obstacles
to clear the way for others.

In the verse, the Hebrew word for leader is *nāśî'*—a prince,
captain, chief, cloud, or leader—it was the person at the head
of the family who held the responsibility for everyone in his
tribe or lineage.

As I read about each leader and what they brought to the
Tabernacle, I was stuck with the thought of how costly the
sacrifice was for each one. Just look at what the first one gave:

His offering was one silver plate weighing 130 shekels, one silver basin
weighing 70 shekels by the shekel of the Sanctuary, both of them filled with
fine flour mixed with oil as a grain offering, one ladle of 10 shekels of

gold filled with incense, one young bull from the herd, one ram, one male
lamb a year old as a burnt offering, one male goat as a sin offering,
and two oxen, five rams, five male goats and five male lambs one year old
to be sacrificed as a fellowship offering. This was the offering
of Nahshon son of Amminadab.

—Numbers 7:13-17 (TLV)

The other eleven leaders brought similar offerings, abundant and extravagant, that required great personal sacrifice. Likewise, leaders do what needs to be done for those they guide. Leaders put their agenda aside and do what's best for the collective. Leaders show up and bring their best. Leaders sacrifice.

Self-Reflection: Leadership is painful and exhilarating. Leadership is costly and rewarding. Leadership is love on display and a beacon in the dark. Leadership is an honor and a gift. The next time a great sacrifice is asked of me, may I remember the One who paid the ultimate price and offer myself willingly—may I go all in, all heart, for Him.

Prayer: Father, thank You for the circles You have placed me in. I have been given more than I deserve. I am grateful. May You find me faithful in all things You have placed within my hands and my influence. It's all from You, all to You, all for Your glory alone. You are good. Your leadership in my life is perfect, and You can be trusted. Amen.

Daily Reading: Numbers 7

YOU WILL RETURN

*And the Israelites set out on their journey from the Wilderness of Sinai,
and the cloud [of the Lord's guiding presence] settled down in the
Wilderness of Paran. So they moved out for the first time in accordance
with the command of the Lord through Moses...So they set out from
the mountain of the Lord (Sinai) three days' journey; and the ark of the
covenant of the Lord went in front of them during the three days' journey
to seek out a resting place for them....And when the ark rested, Moses
said, "Return, O Lord, To the myriad (many) thousands of Israel."*

—Numbers 10:12-13, 33, 36 (AMP)

A great deal of preparation and planning occurred before the
first departure when God determined they were ready to depart
for their first of many journeys. I try to imagine the perspective
of the Israelites. They had to be curious, filled with questions,
and, dare I say, scared.

But something stands out to me: the Ark went ahead to "find
a resting place for them." The Ark represents His presence;
therefore, *He* went ahead. *He* determined the resting place. Then
He guided them by His presence because *He alone knew* the way.

His presence goes before me and guides me. He moves me
from place to place—He tells me when to go or when to "set up

YOUR LAW, MY DELIGHT

camp," and His presence rests. Rest may look like laying hands on someone and praying for them. Rest may look like worship and writing. Rest looks like being settled wherever He guides me.

Since reading this passage, words of a chorus from a song by Brian Doerksen have rattled around in my spirit:

Here oh Lord...have I prepared for you a home
Long have I desired for you to dwell
Here oh Lord...have I prepared a resting place
Here oh Lord...I wait for you alone

The thing I desire most is for God to dwell in me and shine through me. He desires to make His home in me—and in you. No matter where He asks us to go, the promise waiting for us is that He will meet us there.

Self-Reflection: Wherever He sends me, whatever He asks of me, He goes ahead. He prepares the place. And when He tells me to camp, His presence awaits me. God knows what He is doing and where He is going. I can fully trust Him.

Prayer: Father, thank You for Your guiding presence. Thank You for making Your dwelling place within me. You are good. Your leadership in my life is perfect, and You can be trusted. Amen.

Daily Reading: Numbers 8–10

IT'S TOO HEAVY

"I am not able to bear all these people alone, because the burden is too heavy for me. If You treat me like this, please kill me here and now—if I have found favor in Your sight—and do not let me see my wretchedness!" So the Lord said to Moses: "Gather to Me seventy men of the elders of Israel, whom you know to be the elders of the people and officers over them; bring them to the tabernacle of meeting, that they may stand there with you."

—Numbers 11:14-16 (NKJV)

I'm ashamed—but not too proud—to admit I lose my kind sometimes. And no, that's not a typo. It is a realization I have come to about how I respond to stress. If I am not careful, when things are difficult, the hard things harden my attitude.

As I read this passage, I was reminded and encouraged that I am not the only one at the end of my rope at times. When I feel depleted, I am in good company, Moses's to be exact. After the people complained about their provision and lamented their days of slavery, Moses cried out to God. Moses essentially said, *Enough!* Kill them or kill me, but I have had enough!

God's response? He sent burden bearers—seventy of them, to be exact—to stand beside Moses. What a beautiful picture. We are not meant to bear burdens alone!

Self-Reflection: Far too often I bear the burden of work and personal demands mostly alone—not because others won't help, but because I will not or do not ask for it. And when I reach the end of me, when the burdens become too heavy, His quiet voice whispers to my heart—"Gather to Me." He is my helper and my defender. He provides help in my time of need if I just ask.

Prayer: Father, Thank You for mercy. Forgive me for complaining and being unkind. Father—I am weary. Heart weary. Physically weary. Help me. Humbly I present myself, lay my burden at Your feet, and wait. I gather myself to You, my helper and defender. You are good. Your leadership in my life is perfect, and You can be trusted. Amen.

Daily Reading: Numbers 11–13

READING THE REPORT

Then Caleb quieted the people before Moses, and said, "Let us go up at once and take possession, for we are well able to overcome it." But the men who had gone up with him said, "We are not able to go up against the people, for they are stronger than we." And they gave the children of Israel a bad report of the land...So all the congregation lifted up their voices and cried, and the people wept that night. And all the children of Israel complained against Moses and Aaron, and the whole congregation said to them, "If only we had died in the land of Egypt! Or if only we had died in this wilderness! Then Moses and Aaron fell on their faces before all the assembly of the congregation of the children of Israel. But Joshua the son of Nun and Caleb the son of Jephunneh, who were among those who had spied out the land, tore their clothes; and they spoke to all the congregation of the children of Israel, saying: "The land we passed through to spy out is an exceedingly good land. If the Lord delights in us, then He will bring us into this land and give it to us, 'a land which flows with milk and honey.' Only do not rebel against the Lord, nor fear the people of the land, for they are our bread; their protection has departed from them, and the Lord is with us. Do not fear them. And all the congregation said to stone them with stones. Now the glory of the Lord appeared in the tabernacle of meeting before all the children of Israel."

—Numbers 13: 30-32, 14:1-2, 5-10 (NKJV)

This moment of choice had a profound and lasting impact on the Israelites. They had to choose between a good report and a bad report—a report of faith or a report of fear. And after they chose to believe the bad report, they wept all night and complained all day.

The responses to the complaints are interesting to me. Moses and Aaron responded by falling on their faces and worshipping God. Joshua and Caleb responded by tearing their clothes—a sign of grief and sorrow—and tried once again to reason with the Israelites.

Yet the very people who witnessed God's miracles in Egypt, the ones who saw His tangible presence in the form of a cloud by day and a fire by night, who ate of the provision that came from His very hand, and who heard His voice as He spoke to Moses chose to believe one bad report. They chose fear over faith.

I am faced with "reports" of things happening daily, what might happen or supposedly is happening in the world around me. We all are. And each time I hear a report, I am faced with the choice of my response: Will I choose faith or fear? Will I respond with fear that fills my mouth and heart with complaints, weeping, regrets, lamenting, and accusations, or will I bow down in worship, seeking *his* counsel, crying out to Him for His truth?

There is power and impact in our choices. Because the Israelites chose complaint and unbelief, they lost the promise of inheriting the Promised Land and continued their wandering. Unbelief kept them from their inheritance. Unbelief kept them from their destiny! God have mercy on me. What is my unbelief keeping me from!

Self-Reflection: Each report that comes, it's my choice how I read it. May I read the report with a heart of faith. May I have His eyes. May my hope be found in Him alone, not the voices around me.

Prayer: Father, tune my ears and heart to You. Shift the dial. I hear static, and my vision is blurry. But—*you* are good. Your leadership in my life is perfect, and You can be trusted. Help me live fully in that space. Amen.

Daily Reading: Numbers 14–15

POSTURE OF DEFENSE

And they rose up before Moses with some of the children of Israel, two
hundred and fifty leaders of the congregation, representatives of the
congregation, men of renown. They gathered together against Moses and
Aaron, and said to them, "You take too much upon yourselves, for all
the congregation is holy, every one of them, and the Lord is among them.
Why then do you exalt yourselves above the assembly of the Lord?" So
when Moses heard it, he fell on his face; and he spoke to Korah and all his
company, saying, "Tomorrow morning the Lord will show who is His and
who is holy, and will cause him to come near to Him. That one whom He
chooses He will cause to come near to Him."

—Numbers 16:2-5 (NKJV)

Moses heard grumblings and complaints from the Israelites the
moment they left Egypt. It was fairly common. But this time a
group of Israelites had formed a rebellion of sorts.

The Hebrew word for "they rose up" is *qûm*. In this passage,
it indicates a hostile gathering—much like a violent protest that
was gathered or organized suddenly. Three main men (v. 1 and
v. 24) incited 250 men to stand against Moses in an aggressive,
accusatory manner. They were posturing for a battle.

Moses's response? He fell on his face—not out of fear, but
out of humility—showing himself fully dependent on God. It's a
posture mentioned often in Numbers—*nāpal*, prostrate, literally

117

throwing oneself onto the mercy of another. Moses's response to accusations, to violence, and to complaint was to place himself in a posture of complete dependence on God.

Violence runs rampant. Accusations and complaints echo loudly. People rise up in rebellion. How will I respond? I will *nāpal*. Face down. Dependent. Postured to hear His voice and let Him lead.

Self-Reflection: He is my defender. I will look to Him alone to know when it's time to speak or be still. When the enemy's voice rises, I will go low and let God defend me.

Prayer: Father—thank You for Your Word. Thank You for Your mercy and grace. Thank You for Your protection. Help me to trust You more. You are good. Your leadership in my life is perfect, and You can be trusted. Amen.

Daily Reading: Numbers 16–17

A GIFT TO ME

Behold, I Myself have taken your fellow Levites from among the sons of
Israel; they are a gift to you, given (dedicated) to the Lord, to do the service
for the Tent of Meeting (tabernacle).

—Numbers 18:16 (AMP)

Those who look to God for salvation are called to a life of service—it is not for only those in the pulpit.

But—there are those who are called by God set aside specifically to serve the "Tent of Meeting," and those men and women are called "gifts."

I've been thinking a lot lately about the pastors that have influenced us. Having served one closely for twelve years as his assistant, along with serving the network of pastors he led, I have seen the ugly side of church. The side where members disrespect a pastor to his face. The side where a pastor is told, "You no longer belong here." The side where complaints abound because someone did not like the music or the passage from Sunday.

I have also seen the side where a "pastor" used his position to berate and belittle others. Church life—on the "inside"—is not pretty. More than one person tried to talk me out of it, but thankfully I was too stubborn because it was the greatest season of my life.

It is easy to forget that our pastors are humans with hearts and, moreover, they have been specifically set aside by God to do *His* work. And He describes them as His gift to us. I am not in a position now to give my life full time to the ministry like I did in 2001. But I am in a position to serve and love my pastor. I am in a position to pray for him and his wife. I am in a position to encourage him. I am in a position to guard my heart and mind against judgmental thoughts that try to come. I am in a position to participate in the work of the "Tent of Meeting" when I come to its entrance.

In a season full of strife and division in the world around us, guarding the unity of the Body of Christ is crucial and starts with how we honor the spiritual authority God has placed over us. As a member of a church, I'm under my pastor's spiritual authority. The Bible says others will know us by our love, yet so often the church is filled with offense and strife.

Self-Reflection: I am convicted to stand up a little straighter to the tactics of the enemy and love my pastors a little harder. My pastors are a gift from God and should be treated as such.

Prayer: Father, thank You for the pastors that have loved and guided our family. I am so grateful! Give them wisdom to lead according to Your Word and Your will. You are good. Your leadership in my life is perfect, and You can be trusted. Amen.

Daily Reading: Numbers 18–20

BALAAM'S DONKEY

Now the donkey saw the Angel of the Lord standing in the way with His drawn sword in His hand, and the donkey turned aside out of the way and went into the field. So Balaam struck the donkey to turn her back onto the road.... Then the Lord opened the mouth of the donkey, and she said to Balaam, "What have I done to you, that you have struck me these three times?" ... Then the Lord opened Balaam's eyes, and he saw the Angel of the Lord standing in the way with His drawn sword in His hand; and he bowed his head and fell flat on his face.... And Balaam said to the Angel of the Lord, "I have sinned, for I did not know You stood in the way against me. Now therefore, if it displeases You, I will turn back."

—Numbers 22:23, 28, 31, 34 (NKJV)

Balaam's donkey is a popular story in children's churches. A talking donkey is funny imagery! Personally, it is one of our favorites, and we reference it often to remind ourselves if God can use a donkey, He can certainly use us!

But as I was reading it again, two different thoughts came to mind: What if the obstacle I am facing, the thing that feels like a denial or a barrier, is really God's mercy? And why was the angel opposing Balaam?

Three times the angel of the Lord stood in front of the donkey, sword drawn, as a barrier on the road. The first time the donkey responded by turning aside and was struck by Balaam. The second time she pushed herself against a wall, crushing Balaam's foot, and he struck her again. Finally, with the path blocked completely, she just lay down under Balaam and he struck her a third time. Then—God opened her mouth and she spoke, and Balaam's eyes were opened to see the angel opposing him because he had sinned.

In verse 20, there is one small, easily missed word: "if." God instructed Balaam to go and told him what to say *if* he was asked once again. Yet the space between "if" and "went" didn't exist. The space was a choice outside of the will of God. Balaam didn't wait to see "if." He disregarded the conditional "if" and just went.

Each barrier was God's mercy and protection. Each barrier moved Balaam and his donkey to a narrower pathway. He found himself more and more restricted in his movement until finally he was forced to stop. The narrowing, the restriction, served a purpose. It was for Balaam's protection: "And the Angel of the Lord said to him, 'Why have you struck your donkey these three times? Behold, I have come out to stand against you...If she had not turned aside from Me, surely I would also have killed you by now'" (Num. 22:32 - 33 [NKJV]).

I have found myself in the space between "if" and "went" on more than one occasion. I hear His voice, but my anxiety or motives drive me to act outside of His timing or will. The barriers I run up against just might be His mercy. The restrictions I feel might be His protection.

Self-Reflection: The story of Balaam's donkey is a good reminder for me to check my heart for motives or sin, to seek Him about the restrictions and barriers before me, and to submit to His loving hand and perfect timing.

Prayer: Father, thank You for mercy. Forgive me for following my motives and not Your will. Help me to trust You more. You are good. Your leadership in my life is perfect, and You can be trusted. Amen.

Daily Reading: Numbers 21–22

BEAUTIFUL, BLESSED ISRAEL

God is not a man, that He should lie, Nor a son of man, that He should repent. Has He said, and will He not do it? Or has He spoken and will He not make it good and fulfill it? Behold, I have received His command to bless [Israel]. He has blessed, and I cannot reverse it....When Balaam saw that it pleased the Lord to bless Israel, he did not go as he had done each time before [superstitiously] to seek omens and signs [in the natural world], but he set his face toward the wilderness (desert). And Balaam raised his eyes and he saw Israel living in their tents tribe by tribe; and the Spirit of God came on him. He took up his [third] discourse (oracle) and said..."The oracle of the man whose eye is opened [at last, to see clearly the purpose and will of God]...How fair are your tents, O Jacob, And your tabernacles, O Israel!...Blessed [of God] is he who blesses you, And cursed [of God] is he who curses you."

—Numbers 23:19-20; 24:1-3, 5, 9 (AMP)

Beautiful, blessed Israel. I cannot explain why. I do not understand it myself, but I love Israel and the Jewish people. I've been fortunate to go to Israel twice—and both times it was not long enough. Even now I long to be in the Land. On both trips, everywhere I looked, my heart swelled with love and a cry rose within me: *"How beautiful are your tents, oh Israel!"*

We each have things we feel passionately about. and I believe those passions often come from Him. Balaam lifted up his eyes toward the wilderness, and when he saw the tents, God opened Balaam's spiritual eyes to reveal His will. God turned and changed Balaam's heart.

Likewise, I believe God placed the love I have for Israel and His people in my heart. There is a principle in the Word of God surrounding Israel and the Jewish people—His chosen land, His chosen people.

I have heard people in some churches speak of replacement theology—basically saying anywhere the Bible says "Israel," we can replace it with the "church." This is simply not true.

God made a covenant with Abram and confirmed it time and time again. God is not a man that He should lie or change His mind. He doesn't hate Israel—He loves her. He hasn't rejected or cast off the Jewish people—He loves them.

Self-Reflection: To walk fully in His way requires that I love what He loves—and that means Israel and His people. With the rise of antisemitism in the world, this passage burns in my heart. Whatever I face—whatever I encounter—may my eyes be opened to clearly see the purpose and will of God.

Prayer: Father—You are faithful and unchanging. Open my eyes to see Your purpose and Your will so I may respond how You would have me. You are good. Your leadership in my life is perfect, and You can be trusted. Amen.

Daily Reading: Numbers 23–25

Serah, Daughter of Asher, a Warrior

And the name of the daughter of Asher was Serah.

—Numbers 26:46 (NKJV)

What a simple yet powerful verse. The name of one woman mentioned among thousands of men above the age of twenty who were counted as ones who left Egypt and were able to go to war (v. 1–4).

Since she was mentioned in a verse all by herself, she had to be someone of significance!

Curiosity got the best of me, and a quick search revealed two other times she was mentioned—Genesis 46:17 and 1 Chronicles 7:30.

In Genesis 46, she is listed alongside her brothers as one who left with Jacob to journey to Egypt. The chapter lists sixty-nine men and one woman—Serah: "The sons of Asher were Jimnah, Ishuah, Isui, Beriah, and Serah, their sister. And the sons of Beriah were Heber and Malchiel" (Gen. 46:17 [NKJV]).

And we see her in another scenario where once again she is listed alongside of her brothers and among those "fit for battle" (1 Chron. 7:30, 40).

In Hebrew, the name śeraḥ means, literally, "the prince breathed." It also means "abundant." Many theories abound in ancient rabbinical writings and teachings regarding Serah. Some teachings say she never died; others say she was captured up like Elijah. Some teachings say she was the one that broke the news to Jacob about his son Joseph being alive. Some teachings suggest she was Asher's adopted daughter; others say she was his by birth. Some teachings say she is the one that helped Moses find Jacob's bones in order to take his body with them during the Exodus; others say she gave a firsthand account of passing through the Red Sea, describing it like a wall of transparent glass, to rabbis hundreds of years after the Exodus.

I wonder what it was about her character that made her so remarkable. If she had been among those that complained about manna and worshiped an idol, she would not have entered the Promised Land. If she had been among those that believed the bad report of the spies, she would not have entered the Promised Land. For some reason, she was granted an exceptionally long life—she entered Egypt, she left during the Exodus, and she was set to enter the Promised Land after 40 years of wandering in the desert, which is believed to be a time span of at least 250 years.

Either way, whatever stories are true and whatever are legend, the fact is that Serah was a person of value. She was mentioned three times in the Bible. And she was the *only* woman mentioned in both the journey up to Egypt and the journey into the Promised Land. She was counted as one "fit for battle." Serah was a warrior. She was steadfast and faithful. She was valued and loved. She lived an abundant, long life. The Bible doesn't say if she was ever married—but based on the fact that her name was mentioned alone, the overarching belief is that she remained an unmarried virgin throughout her life. Her character alone is what made her remarkable, not a list of accolades—just quiet, unyielding, unwavering strength and faith.

Self-Reflection: Magdala, in Israel, is believed to be the birthplace and city of Mary of Magdalene. The historical site has an atrium with eight pillars designed to honor seven remarkable women of the Bible and one unmarked pillar honoring all women who love God and live by faith. While Serah is not listed on the pillars there, she is listed in the eternal word of God. She was a remarkable woman who's character, tenacity, and longevity inspire me! Serah, daughter of Asher, "the prince's breath," warrior for Him, honored by God.

Prayer: Father, thank You that You love and value women. Thank You for opening my eyes to something and to someone new. Your Word inspires me and transforms me. Give me a warrior's heart, steadfast, unyielding, unwavering. May my life bring honor to You. You are good. Your leadership in my life is perfect, and You can be trusted. Amen.

Daily Reading: Numbers 26–27

RASH WORDS,
SERIOUS CONSEQUENCES

But if she marries while under her vows or if she has bound herself by a rash statement, and her husband hears of it and says nothing about it on the day he hears it, then her vows shall stand and her pledge by which she bound herself shall stand. But if her husband disapproves of her [making her vow or pledge] on the day that he hears of it, then he shall annul her vow which she is under and the rash statement of her lips by which she bound herself; and the Lord will forgive her. . .Every vow and every binding oath to humble herself, her husband may confirm it or her husband may annul it."

—Numbers 30:6-8, 13 (AMP)

When we first married, I was a hot freaking mess. And not in a cute way. I was broken, immature, and an emotional wreck. My wounds spewed forth through my words, mostly aimed at myself.

Rash words. Serious consequences.

Bless my husband. He had been taught the principle here in Numbers—that a husband had the power to reverse the curse of rash words and vows hastily spoken.

The Hebrew word, *mibṭā'*, meaning rash utterance or hasty vow, is used only twice in the Old Testament—both in this chapter—and is derived from the word *bāṭā*, meaning to speak angrily or thoughtlessly. The word *bāṭā* is used in Psalms 106:33 to describe how Moses spoke "recklessly" with his lips because he was angry and in Proverbs 12:18 to compare how words spoken rashly are like thrusts of a sword—in other words, they inflict damage.

In Numbers 30:6, the Hebrew word for bound means "to place in a prison." In other words, rash words—which most often spew out of anger, negative emotion, or a broken and wounded heart—have the power to imprison us. Yikes.

As spouses and parents, we should attune our ears to rashly spoken words we hear uttered. We have tried to be intentional with one another and our children to respond to the rash, harsh words with truth so they do not have the power to bind us or our children. Sometimes that looks like long conversations to discover the pain behind the words. Sometimes it looks like asking what voice they are echoing—the voice of Truth or the voice of the enemy. Sometimes it looks like repentance and restoration, especially if they're just echoing us. And always it looks like praying over and speaking a blessing of truth to replace the lie.

Self-Reflection: Words have power—especially those spoken rashly—because they often are preceded by "I will never" or "I will always" statements that have the power to turn the painful phrase or feeling into a vow. But when confronted with the Truth, when measured against His Word and His promises, we have the power to break curses and shepherd the souls of the people we love the most. May I be ever mindful of the cost of my words and measure them accordingly.

Prayer: Father, bring a crop failure to words I'm unaware that I've sown. Bring them to mind that I might repent and restore. Guard my heart and tongue. May my words bring life and freedom. May my children's words be filled with life and freedom. You are good. Your leadership in my life is perfect, and You can be trusted. Amen.

Daily Reading: Numbers 28–30

THE FINAL STAND: A WAR FOR WORSHIP

The Lord spoke to Moses, saying, "Take vengeance for the Israelites on the Midianites; afterward you will be gathered to your people [in death]." Moses spoke to the people, saying, "Arm men from among you for war, so that they may go against Midian to execute the Lord's vengeance on Midian [for seducing Israel to participate in idolatry]"...Moses sent them, a thousand from each tribe, to the war, and Phinehas the son of Eleazar the priest, to war with them, and the sacred vessels [of the sanctuary] and the trumpets to blow the alarm in his hand.

—Numbers 31:1-3, 6 (AMP)

God gives Moses a final task to accomplish before his death—a war over worship. Twelve thousand men were readied for battle along with one zealous priest—Phinehas—in what would be Moses's final assignment.

I have so many thoughts about this passage, but what comes to mind—rather, *who* comes to mind—is Grandma Purtell.

Grandma Purtell was far from a violent woman in the flesh. Tiny, spunky Trixie wasn't scary to look at to most of the world, but to the demonic realm, she was likely as zealous and as terrifying as Phinehas the Priest, because she was, until her final breath, a worshipper. Worship was her heart. She was zealous for God. She told her nurses about Him the day she drew her last breath. It was her assignment. It was her battlefield.

Moses knew he would die after this battle—not in the battle, but at the conclusion of it. After the twelve thousand were selected, he chose Phinehas, along with holy articles, to accompany them. Since no "general" is mentioned, theologians make the conclusion that Phinehas was the leader of the tribes. Moses sent them to war with instruments of worship (the holy articles and the horn) and a worship leader. In Numbers 25, Phinehas's zealous response turned God's wrath from the Israelites, and as a result, Phinehas was given a covenant of peace:

"Then the Lord spoke to Moses, saying, 'Phinehas the son of Eleazar, the son of Aaron the priest, has turned my wrath away from the Israelites because he was jealous with My jealousy among them, so that I did not destroy the Israelites in My jealousy. Therefore say, "Behold, I give to Phinehas My covenant of peace. And it shall be for him and his descendants after him, a covenant of an everlasting priesthood, because he was jealous (impassioned) for [the unique honor and respect owed to] his God and made atonement for the sons of Israel" (Num. 25:10-13 [AMP]).

I find it interesting that a man—given a covenant of "peace"—led the way into war. It is easy to assume that the passage means peace as we understand it—but the Hebrew translates it more accurately to a "covenant of friendship with God."

A "friend of God"—a worshipper—went first.

Worship led the way. Worship was violent. Worship was loud.

Worship *was* the battle. Worship *won* the war.

God is after my heart at all costs. He is jealous for me and my affections. He will not share me with another. He will not compete against social media, gaming, or whatever else is distracting me. He is after my devotion. There's a war going on in the heavens. I hear the sound of it—the battle cry—coming out of worshippers around the earth.

It is easy to be distracted by the news and everything happening, from the price of gas to the wars on the streets. I'm not saying we should not be informed—we should be so we can pray—but we should not be so consumed that we are distracted from the real battle raging in the heavens and the spiritual world around us—the battle for our hearts and our affections, mine, yours, our family's.

Self-Reflection: There is One alone who is worthy, and He won't share His worship with another. The true battle is against the spirits of darkness trying to seduce us away. I hear the cry. I hear the sound. I'm picking up my instruments. I'm laying down my distractions. I'm all in.

Prayer: Father—give me the heart of Phinehas, a zeal for You that consumes me. Remove distractions. Convict my heart of what barriers exist that I cannot see. You alone are worthy of my devotion and worship. You alone are good. Your leadership in my life is perfect, and You alone can be trusted. Amen.

Daily Reading: Numbers 31–32

REGRETS—
MY IDOL WORSHIP

Now the Lord spoke to Moses in the plains of Moab by the Jordan, across
from Jericho, saying, "Speak to the children of Israel, and say to them:
'When you have crossed the Jordan into the land of Canaan, then you
shall drive out all the inhabitants of the land from before you, destroy all
their engraved stones, destroy all their molded images, and demolish all
their high places...But if you do not drive out the inhabitants of the land
from before you, then it shall be that those whom you let remain shall be
irritants in your eyes and thorns in your sides, and they shall harass you
in the land where you dwell.'"

—Numbers 33:50-52, 15 (NKVJ)

There were three separate directives for the Israelites to follow
when they first possessed the long-awaited Promised Land: drive
out, destroy, and demolish.

First, they were to *yāraš* the inhabitants—in other words,
drive out by force whatever was there so that it could be fully
possessed. Second, they were directed to *ābad*—to completely
destroy or vanquish beyond all recognition all *maśkît* and
massēkâ, the carvings, engraved stones, figure, imaginations
image, idols, pictures and molded images (gods like the golden

calf). Finally, they were instructed to *bāmâ*—to demolish all the high places or elevated stands where Baal and other gods were worshipped.

The Israelites stood on the edge of possessing a long-awaited promise, yet God knew the promise could become a "thorn in their sides" if they did not fully possess it. There was work to do before inhabiting the promise.

Standing on the precipice of a promise myself, being able to see a glimmer of the hope of what will be, this resonated with me.

I have a "high" place in my heart and mind, a place that has become like engraved stones that take up room in my heart—it's a list I keep. A list of regrets a mile long. It might not be written, but it is engraved in my mind. I carry regret around like baggage and hold to memories like idols—lamenting the past, wondering what might have been. The Lord spoke to me that my list of regrets, those things I lament, which I can pull up in my mind in an instant, are like engraved images, unwelcome inhabitants, and high places of false worship.

Self-Reflection: Each bend in the road led us to the place we are today. And to fully possess all the gifts, lessons, pain, and promises that He has for us in *this* season, we must take off and completely destroy the "masks" we wear and carry like armor from one season into the next. We have to drive out, destroy, and demolish *everything* that opposes Him—and regrets oppose His goodness.

Prayer: Father, You've heard my lament. You've seen my list. Forgive me. I repent of the lament. Father, I ask that You tear it up in my mind—the what might've, could've, should've been. I say I trust You—then regrets leave me doubting. Forgive me. Heal my mind and my heart. Take my regrets and give me Your truth. You are good. Your leadership in my life is perfect, and You can be trusted. Amen.

Daily Reading: Numbers 33–34

CITIES OF REFUGE

Now among the cities which you will give to the Levites, you shall appoint six cities of refuge, to which a manslayer may flee.

—Numbers 35:6 (NKJV)

Cities of refuge—physical places of safety, free of judgment and punishment—were established by God in the beginning. Set among the Levites—or lead priests and worship leaders—these cities were asylums where people wrongly accused could flee to in order to find protection until a trial was convened. It's a beautiful picture, really, to think that God chose to prepare a place among His ministers where people could be protected when they were wrongly accused.

I hear accusations and judgments all the time in all areas. Sinful natures tend to "assume" someone is guilty until proven innocent instead of the concept at the foundation of our justice system—innocent until proven guilty.

One of the greatest gifts and lessons I learned from a mentor at work is to API: assume positive intent. Assume the best, not the worst. Give people a chance to tell you the other side of the story. Listen and learn. Seek to understand. Come to the conversation curious.

From the beginning, redemption was His plan, seen so clearly in the fact that He set aside cities of refuge. I'm guessing God thought His ministers were the best ones to give API to the wrongly accused—the best ones to provide a place free of judgment and ensure their safety, both physically and spiritually.

In a world full of fear and wrong assumptions, may I be a city of refuge for loved ones and strangers alike. After all, I'm a carrier of His presence and a minister unto Him; therefore, I should be a place free of judgment, free of punishment, and free of shame. I should welcome the wrongly accused and give them some API. I shouldn't jump to wrong conclusions. I should forgive. I should love. Whether my loved ones, family, friends, colleagues, or strangers—it's not my place to sit in judgment as I have done so often and by nature tend to do so still. Father, forgive me.

Self-Reflection: Love is my highest calling—after all, Yeshua became my city of refuge, my safe place to run to, free of judgment and punishment.

Prayer: Father—I repent and ask for forgiveness for standing in judgment when it is Your place alone. Thank You for making a way for me—a safe place in Your Son. What beautiful imagery to bring hope to my soul. Make my heart and my home a place free of accusation and judgment, a city of refuge and asylum where others are positioned to find You for You alone are the Redeemer. You are good. Your leadership in my life is perfect, and You can be trusted. Amen.

Daily Reading: Numbers 35–36

YET FOR ALL THIS...

Yet for all this you did not trust in Adonai your God.

—Deuteronomy 1:32 (TLV)

Deuteronomy—the fifth book of the Torah and Moses's final three sermons of his life, sermons meant to prepare the Israelites to enter and inhabit the Promised Land. As he opens his final words, he begins by reminding them of the many things God has done. It is kind of like watching a highlight reel.

What struck me in this simple verse above: "yet for all this you did not trust."

I have been meditating recently on what God has done for me—*and there is so much!* I could fill a book with the numerous testimonies from my own life of ways God has healed me, guided me, protected me, and cared for me.

Yet...still, at times, I doubt, I question, I worry, I complain. Why? Because I lack vision, I believe a bad report, I complain, and I have a short memory when my "feelings" are involved.

Self-Reflection: Sometimes I need a Moses to remind me of the "for all this." Sometimes I just need to remind myself because when I do, I'm overwhelmed at His goodness to me.

Prayer: Father, You have been so kind to me, more kind than I deserve. You are the only One worthy of worship and devotion. You are good. Your leadership in my life is perfect. I trust You. Amen.

Daily Reading: Deuteronomy 1–2

THE GOOD LIFE

Only take heed to yourself, and diligently keep yourself, lest you forget the things your eyes have seen, and lest they depart from your heart all the days of your life. And teach them to your children and your grandchildren. . . Take heed to yourselves, lest you forget the covenant of the Lord your God which He made with you, and make for yourselves a carved image in the form of anything which the Lord your God has forbidden you. For the Lord your God is a consuming fire, a jealous God. . . You shall therefore keep His statutes and His commandments which I command you today, that it may go well with you and with your children after you, and that you may prolong your days in the land which the Lord your God is giving you for all time.

—Deuteronomy 4:9, 23-24, 40 (NKJV)

The majority of parents I know share one common desire: that life will go well for our kids.

The Hebrew word used in verse 40 for "go well with" is *yāṭaḇ*—and in this passage it means to be well for, to be well with, and to go well with. The verse could say: "You shall therefore keep His statutes and His commandments which I command you today *that it may be well for, that it may be well with, and that it may go well with you and with your children after you.*"

In other words—may things happen or progress in a positive manner throughout their lives, constantly moving forward and improving over time, that they would be strong in mind, body, and spirit. May they have a good life—not perfect, but a good (morally excellent, virtuous, righteous, satisfactory in quality and quantity) life. Finally, something we can all agree on and aspire to!

Now for the how. Thankfully God gave us the answer: take heed of ourselves to obey His commands and teach them to our children. Take heed and obey.

The Hebrew word šāmar is used four times in the passage above and means to "hedge about with thorns," to protect, to guard, to observe, to set watch at—like a watchman at a gate. I love this word and this visual imagery. Only things of high value or worth are guarded and protected with such diligence. To position our children (or grandchildren) as best as we can for a good life, we must start with guarding ourselves—specifically guarding and protecting our relationship with Him. They say absence makes the heart grow fonder—but I wager that is true only if you guard your heart while the one you love is away. We have to nurture relationships with those we love whether we are physically with them or not. It is the same with God.

Self-Reflection: When we miss days in His presence and prioritize other things over Him, our hearts and minds wander and tend to forget. It's only by engaging the object of our affections with intention and resolve that we can nurture the relationship.

In Word War I, a guard who was caught sleeping on duty faced death by firing squad. Being a watchman is serious business— am I up to the task? May He find me alert, attentive, and ready for duty.

Prayer: Father—thank You for Your Word and Your wisdom. Teach me to number my days. You are good. Your leadership in my life is perfect, and You can be trusted. Amen.

Daily Reading: Deuteronomy 3–4

WHY DO YOU LOVE ME!

For you are a holy people [set apart] to the Lord your God; the Lord your God has chosen you out of all the peoples on the face of the earth to be a people for His own possession [that is, His very special treasure]. The Lord did not love you and choose you because you were greater in number than any of the other peoples, for you were the fewest of all peoples. But because the Lord loves you and is keeping the oath which He swore to your fathers, the Lord has brought you out with a mighty hand and redeemed (bought) you from the house of slavery, from the hand of Pharaoh king of Egypt. Therefore know [without any doubt] and understand that the Lord your God, He is God, the faithful God, who is keeping His covenant and His [steadfast] loving kindness to a thousand generations with those who love Him and keep His commandments.

—Deuteronomy 7:6-9 (AMP)

Why do you love me! It is a question I have uttered more than once in my lifetime because I was unable to fathom why someone would love me. I have screamed it in anger and whispered it through tears—both sounds rising from a broken place deep within me, as I was convinced that I wasn't good enough for love and certainly didn't deserve it.

"Why?" is the question we often want answered more than any other because it is tied to our emotions and helps make sense of a mysterious situation on a rational level.

God answered the why in His Word: Why does He love me? Because He chose to love me, and He is keeping His covenant with Abraham, Isaac, and Jacob. It is because of His choice and His word. It is that simple.

There was a moment when Vance and I were first engaged that I begged him not to marry me. Standing outside of his red truck in front of the All Nations House of Prayer, I screamed the question "Why do you love me!" His answer was profound: "I choose to love you not because of who you are today but because of who the Holy Spirit is making you." Vance made a choice early on to love me. It cost him relationships and pain, but he did not back down. When we spoke our vows, I said that he had been a steady example of God's love for me, and it is still true. Earthly love is a choice we make—it can be costly, painful, transformative, and amazing.

Self-Reflection: God's love for me is so much more profound and transformative. His love is all-encompassing and gracious. His love is jealous and kind. His love is eternal. His love is unchanging and unconditional. I can rest in the confidence of knowing that He loves me because He chooses to—it's just that simple and that profound.

Prayer: Father—thank You for loving me. Thank You for answering the "why?" of my heart. You are faithful and good. You are kind and forgiving. You alone are worthy of praise. Your leadership in my life is perfect, and You can be trusted. Amen.

Daily Reading: Deuteronomy 5–7

A GOOD LAND

And you shall remember [always] all the ways which the Lord your God has led you these forty years in the wilderness, so that He might humble you and test you, to know what was in your heart (mind), whether you would keep His commandments or not. He humbled you and allowed you to be hungry and fed you with manna, [a substance] which you did not know, nor did your fathers know, so that He might make you understand [by personal experience] that man does not live by bread along but by every word that proceeds out of the mouth of the Lord...Therefore, know in your heart (be fully cognizant) that the Lord your God disciplines and instructs you just as a man disciplines and instructs his son. Therefore, you shall keep the commandments of the Lord your God, to walk [that is, to live each and every day] in His ways and fear [and worship] Him [with awe-filled reverence and profound respect]. For the Lord your God is bringing you into a good land, a land of brooks of water, of fountains and springs, flowing forth in valleys and hills."

—Deuteronomy 8:2-3, 5-7 (AMP)

When we left Grand Prairie in 2003, we headed into our personal wilderness, and Trinity Fellowship Church in Tyler, Texas welcomed us with open arms. While we were there, someone prophesied over us that they saw us with suitcases in our hands. I tilted my head back and loudly cried, "Nooooooo!"—I did not want that. Tyler was home. They carried us through miscarriages and more. I wanted roots, but God had an assignment for our family, so we moved again—Hurst to Grand Prairie, then to our beloved Kentucky home, then back to Fort Worth, Canton, and finally home to Hurst again. We have so many wonderful friends and memories in each place!

In 2022 I felt in my spirit that our wilderness season was almost over. I did not know all of the places we would go during our marriage, but I knew in my heart that the wandering would come to an end at some point. I felt a little like the Israelites receiving the last instructions from Moses as we prepared to step into the Jordan to cross over before each major move. Every move and each step along the way made me who I have become, and I can confidently say He has brought me, Vance, and our children into a good, good land where we walk in His fullness and provision physically, spiritually, and emotionally.

Self-Reflection: Even when we cannot see the way before us, He is leading us to a good land. His promises are sure. His word is true. We will experience both gifts and losses along the way. In the words of Dr. Seuss, I will not "cry because it's over—I'll smile because it happened." Whatever comes, whenever it comes, I will be ready for it—and I am unpacking my suitcases.

Prayer: Father, You hold our hearts. You know the sorrow we feel at the end of this season and the anticipation I have for the next. Give me wisdom to walk in your ways. Help me know how to encourage our family to continue to chase You passionately at every turn. My heart longs for home and for deep roots—may I find my home in You alone. You are good. Your leadership in my life is perfect, and You can be trusted. Amen.

Daily Reading: Deuteronomy 8–10

CLINGY

*You shall walk after the Lord your God and you shall fear [and worship]
Him [with awe-filled reverence and profound respect], and you shall keep
His commandments and you shall listen to His voice, and you shall serve
Him, and cling to Him.*

—Deuteronomy 13:4 (AMP)

Clingy. I do not like it. At all. I love my personal space, and
for some reason, "clingy" makes me uncomfortable. It feels
awkward to me.

Perhaps that is why this passage was like a slap to the face—
He wants me to serve Him and to *cling* to Him. What! But
Lord—I do not like clingy!

The Hebrew word for cling is *dābaq* and is more accurately
translated as to cleave to, to stay close to, to stick to or stick with,
or to follow closely behind. It's the same word used to describe
how Ruth responded to Naomi when given the choice to leave
her mother-in-law. Ruth held fast to her—refusing to leave her
side (Ruth 1:14). It's also the word used to describe how a man
shall cleave to his wife in marriage (Gen. 2:24).

The Lord is stirring up my heart with this imagery and the
feeling it invokes in my heart. Why does the feeling of someone
hanging onto me invoke strong feelings!

In the quiet space of waiting, He answered those questions for me and revealed a lie I did not realize I had embraced—clinging to someone is a sign of weakness.

As a woman who has experienced abuse, somewhere along the way I told myself I would not allow myself to be truly and totally dependent on another person because it puts me in a vulnerable position. My entire life, I have fought against any perception, sign, or hint of weakness in me, and for some reason, I equated "clingy" with being weak. Therefore, stubbornness became a shield I used to fend off anything or anyone that was clingy—physically or emotionally.

In the quietness with Him, God lovingly convicts me. I rebel against the physical feeling clinginess invokes (heaviness) and the emotion that it awakens in me (fear). I do not like weakness at all—perceived or real. I do not want to be dependent or indebted. I do not want to "owe" someone. Yet—I do.

I owe Someone a debt I could not pay, so He paid it. And in return, He asks me to come in close, close enough that I can touch Him, close enough that I may step on His heels, close enough that I can hear His whisper, and close enough that He can catch me when I stumble from exhaustion.

During a word study for this passage, I discovered something interesting. Our modern English word "climb" is derived from both the Old English word *climban* and from the West Germanic *klimban*—meaning to "go up by clinging," which made me think about Alathia. She loves to climb trees because things just look different—the light shining through the leaves, the things around her, it all looks different when she's perched high in the branches as opposed to having her feet on the ground. Perhaps that's the key to shifting my perspective and thoughts—I must "go up by clinging." Intimacy with God and intimacy with my husband require clinging physically, spiritually, and emotionally.

Self-Reflection: Instead of rebelling against the feeling, I will endeavor to embrace the feeling it evokes as a reminder of the strength I find in clinging to Him because His strength is made perfect in my weakness.

Prayer: Father—thank You for how You lovingly convict me. Heal the place in my heart that You've revealed. You are good. You are gracious and kind. Your leadership in my life is perfect, and I trust You with the broken places in my mind and in my heart. Amen.

Daily Reading: Deuteronomy 11–13

BRIGHTEN UP

You shall rejoice before the Lord your God, you and your son and your daughter, your male servant and your female servant, the Levite who is within your gates, the stranger and the fatherless and the widow who are among you, at the place where the Lord your God chooses to make His name abide.

—Deuteronomy 16:11 (NKJV)

The phrase "you shall rejoice" conjures up all kinds of images in my mind (dancing, tambourines, etc.) and is not something that has always come naturally to me. As a highly emotive person, my feelings rule my face and my responses far too often. But with this passage, I learned a new meaning of the word "rejoice," and I love it: to brighten up.

The Hebrew word for the phrase "and you shall rejoice" is śāmaḥ ', and it means to brighten up, to cheer up, to be glad; to have, make joy(ful).

In other words, the verse could read, "You shall brighten up before the Lord your God." I love that!

I've struggled at times throughout my life to "feel" joyful. Even when I was a child, my parents could always read my mood with one glance at my face. I would be terrible at poker because the "poker face" doesn't exist in me. If I feel happy, it is clear in my countenance. If I am mad, that is obvious too. Though I have improved somewhat in that area as I have aged, how I am feeling is still fairly obvious when you look at me.

But as I reread this passage, He spoke these words to me: "*Let My presence brighten your countenance.*" In the King James Version, Psalms 34:5 says, "They looked unto him, and were lightened: And their faces were not ashamed." Other versions use the word "radiant."

Rejoicing is not seen in how loud I sing or dance or shake the tambourine. Rejoicing is seen in my countenance. When I spend time with Him and look at Him, when I meditate on His goodness, His holiness, His righteousness, His sovereignty, His nature, I cannot help but brighten up. His *presence* transforms my heart, which in turn brightens up my face!

Self-Reflection: When I have a revelation of *who* He is, it's impossible to remain the same. Perhaps the "facelift" I need is to sit a little longer in His presence until I brighten up.

Prayer: Father—I love how You speak to me! You speak the language of my heart. No one knows me better than You. You bring me such joy. I am so grateful You redeemed me. I am overwhelmed at the realization once again that *you choose me.* May my face and life be a reflection of Your glory. You are good. Your leadership in my life is perfect, and You can be trusted. Amen.

Daily Reading: Deuteronomy 14–16

FOR DANA

Now it shall come about when he sits on the throne of his kingdom, he shall write for himself a copy of this law on a scroll in the presence of the Levitical priests. And it shall be with him and he shall read it all the days of his life, so that he may learn to fear [and worship] the Lord his God [with awe-filled reverence and profound respect].

—Deuteronomy 17:18-19 (AMP)

Her name was Dana. We struck up a random conversation one rainy September morning in Terminal E over a canceled flight. With hours to spare, we headed to Chili's and talked as if we were old friends. Somewhere along the way, I pulled out my favorite purple Bible. It was the one I carried the most. She asked me more questions than I'd been asked by anyone in a long time, and I was thankful to have pages of sermon notes scribbled in the margins for reference.

Back at the gate, we continued our dialogue, and as I continued answering her questions, she kept leaning in closer and closer to see what I was reading from. I told her about David, Ruth, Esther, and Daniel. On and on, turning page after page, then she saw it—the red words. Touching the page, she leaned across me and asked, "What is that? Why are all of those in red?"

I explained they were Jesus's words. She was speechless for the first time in hours. Jesus's words on a page—how could that be! Knowing we were close to boarding, I explained how she could have access to the Father through His Son and taught her a quick prayer. I explained salvation as best I could and placed my Bible in her hands as we stood. She tried to refuse it, but I insisted.

Though she was raised in church, she had never seen—much less held—a Bible, the written Word of God, and as I watched her walk away with my purple Bible clutched to her chest, the picture gripped me and convicted me to my core. The look on her face and the tears in her eyes, combined with the gentle way she hugged my Bible, made it clear that she treasured the Word of God. In that moment she *got it*. I do not know that I had ever beheld—much less *held*—the Word of God with the reverence she expressed that day.

I texted Dana for the next several months after that chance encounter. She would ask me to pray for her, and we would talk about what she had read. She would send me pictures of what she saw in the margins and ask about notes. She even sent me pictures of her notes next to mine. Then the texts stopped, and her phone went silent. Over a year went by before I finally heard from her again.

Dana asked to meet in person, and since I happened to be in Charlotte for work, it was perfect timing. I do not remember where we met or what we ate, but over an extended meal, Dana explained where she had been. She had traveled out of the country to visit her son when something she took with her—which ended up being illegal in that country—landed her in a work prison. Separated from her family, unable to communicate, and living on just bread and water, she told me of the many dark nights she lay on her dirty little cot with a thin blanket wrapped around her, desperate for warmth and desperately lonely. She described the fear that consumed her while listening to rodents scurrying about. And in the silence, staring into the dark, she began to remember the Bible stories I told her, she began to see pictures of the red words on the pages that she read and the notes in the margins, and she remembered how to pray. Eventually a priest came, and she asked for an English Bible. She somehow got it, and she began to devour the Word. It wasn't the same soft Bible she had come to love, but it had the same red words. She was released after some legal assistance and had found her way home about a month before we met.

She told me the one thing that sustained her was the Word of God. After I gave her the Bible, she read it daily until her trip. Then, when food was scarce and the situation absolutely devastating and hopeless, His Word was literal food for her. We lost touch shortly after that night, but meeting her changed me.

She is who I thought of when I read this passage. The Word of God was with her, and through the reading of His Word, she was transformed and sustained. She had a profound respect for God and His Word from the moment she beheld it, and it changed her.

Self-Reflection: People and experiences may move us emotionally and chance encounters like mine with Dana leave a lasting imprint, but He alone has the power to transform and sustain us. The more I read His word, the more I learn about Him. The more I learn about Him, the more I am in awe of Him. And the more behold Him, the more I become like Him.

Prayer: Father, thank You for Dana. Thank You for trusting me to be a carrier of Your word to her. You see her now—bless her, I pray. Father—forgive me for treating Your word so casually. Put a reverence in my heart for Your word and Your presence. Transform me into Your image. Put Your word in my heart and mind. You are good. Your leadership in my life is perfect, and You can be trusted. Amen.

Daily Reading: Deuteronomy 17–20

THE BEST NEIGHBOR

You shall not see your brother's donkey or
his ox fall down along the road,
and hide yourself from them;
you shall surely help him lift them up again.

—Deuteronomy 22:4 (NKJV)

God fashioned our hearts for relationships—relationships with our spouse, our family (immediate and extended), and the community He places us in. Ecclesiastes says two are better than one, and Genesis states that man shall leave his father and mother and cleave to his wife. We are not designed to live in silos.

Community is what our hearts long for. True community, a place where we can live in close relationships with others as we help and support one another along the way. When we do so, when we work with another person to carry their burden, it's just easier—and sometimes it's fun. He designed us that way!

Many "good" neighbors come to mind from Tyler to Grand Prairie to Kentucky to Fort Worth—but one neighbor stands out in my mind. Chris and Amber were our neighbors in Lexington when we first moved to Kentucky. While I do not want to offend other good neighbors we have had, the Risalvatos were special!

We borrowed sugar from one another, shared spontaneous meals, and even dressed up like cows for free chicken at Chick-fil-A together. Amber gave Alathia shots in the early days of her diagnosis and kept our kids when I was sick. Chris helped me buy my Honda that I still love and drive. And one fall, we spent *hours* untangling the Christmas tree lights. We shared laughter and tears. We did life together. The season was short—but the impact on our hearts was not.

That is what and who I think of when I read this passage. When someone is in need, God asks me to step in to lend a hand and to walk alongside them until they are back on their feet, able to continue their journey. That's what the Risalvatos did for us. Likewise, we should not ignore those in need and blindly walk past them. My personal mission in life is to leave people better than I found them—to do something to leave others inspired and more "lifted up" in their hearts—and fulfilling my mission requires that I sometimes leave my comfort zone, setting aside my plans if need be to help lift them up again.

Self-Reflection: God sets the lowly in families, and when we needed one fourteen hours from "home," He gave us the Risalvatos, whom we loved like family. No matter where He calls us or my children, He has a place for us. Family is His gift and provision.

Prayer: Father—thank You for Chris and Amber. What a gift they were to us! Cause Your face to shine on them, Amelia, and Owen. Father, help me to see what You see in those around me and give me wisdom to know how to help those in need. You are good. Your leadership in my life is perfect, and You can be trusted. Amen.

Daily Reading: Deuteronomy 21–23

BROUGHT
OUT TO BRING IN

Then we cried out to the Lord God of our fathers, and the Lord heard our voice and looked on our affliction and our labor and our oppression. So the Lord brought us out of Egypt with a mighty hand and with an outstretched arm, with great terror and with signs and wonders. He has brought us to this place and has given us this land, 'a land flowing with milk and honey'; and now, behold, I have brought the first fruits of the land which you, O Lord, have given me. Then you shall set it before the Lord your God, and worship before the Lord your God. So you shall rejoice in every good thing which the Lord your God has given to you and your house, you and the Levite and the stranger who is among you.

—Deuteronomy 26:7-11 (NKJV)

Deuteronomy is the story of the Israelites leaving Egypt for the Promised Land, their journey through the wilderness, the giving of the Ten Commandments, and the death of Moses. The journey through the wilderness is full of symbolism and lessons that resonate deeply with me, especially in light of our multiple moves. Whether it is a physical move or a spiritual one, I have found that God has often moved me *out* of one place so He could move me *into* another. Deuteronomy 6:23 says this: "He is moving us out to bring us into position to fulfill His work in and through us."

While meditating on this passage, I heard God's whisper quietly to my soul: *"Oppression is just labor pain birthing you into a new season."*

As I look back at major transitions in our life, I am amazed at how they feel like labor—uncomfortable, painful, scary, unsure, exhausting—yet on the other side of the transition, there have been times of great rejoicing, maybe not immediately, but the rejoicing always came.

When a child is born, people often say a mother has "amnesia" —she is somehow able to forget the painful experience in the afterglow of birth and would do it all over again. New parents are one of my favorite things to witness—the unadulterated *joy*, the look of love plastered on weary faces as they gaze at one another and the baby in their arms, is a beautiful, remarkable sight. Every bit of pain, every moment of morning sickness, every ounce of sacrifice worth it in that single moment when their baby is placed in their arms.

I have been privileged to give birth to babies both into heaven and into my arms. With Randal and Alathia, the experience above holds true—I forgot about the pain the moment they were in my arms. But when a child is lost to miscarriage, the grief is often silent and there's no amnesia for the pain. While it may dull over time, they never fully leave your heart. I still hold my babies in my heart, wondering who they would be today and grieving that Alathia never experienced being a big sister, which has long been a desire of her heart. But even in the losses, there is rejoicing. It took me a long time to bring that offering to Him, and when I did, it was a true sacrifice, but rejoicing did come eventually.

It is interesting to me that just as there are signs of physical labor, signs have always preceded our major life transitions, and after thirteen major moves, we have learned to pay attention to the rhythm and signs. After our most recent move, I was intentional in taking time to rest and recover, and in doing so, I am reminded that being birthed into a new season can be painful, exciting, scary, exhausting, joyful, exhilarating, and grievous too.

Self-Reflection: We can rest in the truth that there are good things ahead for us. May we be found rejoicing in the days ahead because He moved us out in order to bring us into a position to fulfill His work in and through us.

Prayer: Father, thank You for the season of loving and serving the Purtells, and thank You for your provision for them and for us. Thank You for preparing a place for us in this season. We trust Your hand to lead, position, and mature us. Give us hearts to receive all You have to teach us. You are good. Your leadership in my life is perfect, and You can be trusted. Amen.

Daily Reading: Deuteronomy 24–27

SECRET KEEPER

The secret things belong to the Lord our God, but those things which are revealed belong to us and to our children forever, that we may do all the words of this law.

—Deuteronomy 29:29 (NKJV)

We raised our kids with the idea that secrets should not be kept. Yet, here in this passage, we learn that secret things belong to God. I have been pondering what secrets those might be—yet I know His ways are beyond my understanding.

I am reminded of something Pastor Olen used to say about God's Word. We can read the same thing over and over again, and each time we can see and learn something different. Those, I think, are the secrets that belong to Him, the truths in His word hidden to me before yet now revealed.

I have a very dear friend who knows many secrets about me—hidden fears and things I have revealed to her because of the friendship and trust we have intentionally cultivated over time through talking, listening, laughing, crying, and just spending time together. The more time we spent together, the more I began to trust her and the more I revealed.

Secrets are shared with those we are close to—not with our acquaintances. I think it is like that with God. The more we spend time with Him, the more we listen to and converse with Him, the more we cultivate our relationship with Him and intentionally pursue Him, the more He reveals Himself to us. And that which is revealed to us now belongs to us and our children.

One of my favorite movies says it this way: "My father told me it takes the glory of God to conceal a matter. And it takes the honor of Kings to search it out" (*Hadassah—One Night with the King*, based on Proverbs 25:2).

The Word says that His eyes roam throughout the whole earth to see whose hearts are fully His so that He might strengthen hearts fully committed to and loyal to Him (2 Chron. 16:9). I believe God desires to reveal Himself to us in order to strengthen and sustain us.

Self-Reflection: The question I must ask myself is this: Does He find me trustworthy and able to carry, guard, and shepherd the secrets He longs to reveal to me? When His eyes find me, may I be found as one loyal to Him.

Prayer: Father—thank You for speaking to me through Your Word, and thank You for placing people in my life who teach me about You. Father, make my heart loyal to You. Root out that which is not pleasing to You. Draw me close to You so that I may know the secrets of Your heart for me and my family. You are good. Your leadership in my life is perfect, and You can be trusted. Amen.

Daily Reading: Deuteronomy 28–29

CHOOSE WISELY

*And the Lord your God will circumcise your heart and the hearts of your
descendants [that is, He will remove the desire to sin from your heart],
so that you will love the Lord your God with all your heart and all your
soul, so that you may live [as a recipient of His blessing]...I call heaven
and earth as witnesses against you today, that I have set before you life and
death, the blessing and the curse; therefore, you shall choose life in order that
you may live, you and your descendants, by loving the Lord your God,
by obeying His voice, and by holding closely to Him; for He is your life
[your good life, your abundant life, your fulfillment] and the length of
your days, that you may live in the land which the Lord promised (swore)
to give to your fathers, to Abraham, Isaac, and Jacob.*

—Deuteronomy 30:6, 19-20 (AMP)

People that know our family well know that Alathia and I can
quote the entire movie Ever After. It is annoying and hilarious.
The queen says near the end of the movie, "Choose your words
wisely, madam. For they may be your last." That quote is what
came to mind when I read this passage—it was her voice in my
head saying to "choose wisely," my dear.

God places a choice before me: life or death, good or evil.
And my choice does not affect me alone—it affects my children

and their children. My choice determines if we will walk in His promises. There is no middle ground. Life and good are tied directly to obedience. Evil and death are tied directly to disobedience. It seems like a fairly simple formula—until our hearts are distracted and drawn away. Obedience matters. Period.

Self-Reflection: Something I have heard from my husband and pastor often is a truth that applies here: what we behold, we become. The more we behold Him, the more we become like Him. The more we become like Him, the more we see Him. The more we see Him, the more we draw close to Him. The more we draw close to Him, the more we love Him. The more we love Him, the more we obey Him. And the more we obey Him, the more we live a life pleasing to Him. In the end that's the key to a good life, and it's what I really want—to live a life pleasing Him.

Prayer: Father, thank You for Your mercy. Thank You for how You draw me and pursue me. Thank You for forgiveness and grace. Make my life pleasing to You. You are good. Your leadership in my life is perfect, and You can be trusted. Amen.

Daily Reading: Deuteronomy 30–31

MOSES—MAY HIS MEMORY BE A BLESSING

Then Moses went up from the plains of Moab to Mount Nebo,
to the top of Pisgah, which is across from Jericho. And the Lord showed
him all the land of Gilead as far as Dan. . . Then the Lord said to him,
"This is the land of which I swore to give Abraham, Isaac, and Jacob,
saying, 'I will give it to your descendants.' I have caused you to see it with
your eyes, but you shall not cross over there." So Moses the servant of the
Lord died there in the land of Moab, according to the word of the Lord.
And He buried him in a valley in the land of Moab, opposite Beth Peor;
but no one knows his grave to this day. Moses was one hundred and
twenty years old when he died. His eyes were not dim nor his
natural vigor diminished.

—Deuteronomy 34:1, 4-7 (NKJV)

For many years I envisioned Moses as a weak man—but when I read the Bible chronologically, it gave me a new perspective on him. Moses was far from weak.

Moses had physical strength and self-discipline. He boldly went before Pharaoh ten times. He endured *two* forty-day fasts—one before the golden calf and one after. He took all of the instructions God gave him on the mountain to build the

Tabernacle and saw it through to completion.

Moses was also a humble man. He heeded his father in law's counsel and appointed judges. He received God's correction and discipline without argument.

Moses was a worshipper—time and time again, he prostrated himself before God when he did not know what to do, and he communed with God. His countenance glowed from being in God's presence, and he talked to God face-to-face and lived.

Yes—Moses missed it, multiple times. He murdered an Egyptian, then fled for his life and hid in a foreign land until God called him out. And when God called him, Moses argued with God about his physical abilities.

And the biggest miss, Moses did not hallow God before the Israelites when he responded from his flesh and struck the rock instead of speaking to it, and he paid a high price. God told Moses he would not receive the promise because he did not hallow Him—yet Moses kept going. Moses continued to meet with God face-to-face, he kept worshipping, and he kept leading. He did not give up, and he did not stop even though he knew he would never inherit the promise. Mentally, it had to be hard!

Moses made a succession plan. Joshua was appointed and anointed as the one to lead the Israelites into the Promised Land. Moses then gave final instructions—and warnings—to the Israelites, thirty-four chapters' worth, before he finished with a song for the people and prophetic word to each tribe.

And when it was time, when he had completed all God had for him to do, Moses, the murderer turned leader of the great Exodus, breathed his last and was hidden *by* God.

The picture of Moses's death wrecks my heart. I can imagine Moses with a smile on his face as he took in the beauty of the land, then beheld the face of God one last time. I wonder if Moses prostrated himself before the Lord one final time, as an act of worship, while he breathed his last or if he clung to God in death. I can picture God lifting Moses and carrying him to his final resting place—known only to God—almost as if God embraced Moses one final time, like the imagery in Psalms 91—hidden under His wings.

Moses was a man of incredible strength and character. Though once insecure, he died full of "natural vigor" and strength. Moses, the murderer, died as a friend of God. He finished his life forgiven, accepted, and fulfilled.

Proverbs 10:7 says, "The memory of the righteous is a blessing" (TLV). It is customary to say "may his/her memory be a blessing" when a Jewish person passes or when it is the anniversary of their death and for the person's name to be followed by z"l —the shorthand for *zikhronah livrakah*, or blessed memory in Hebrew— may the memory of that person and their good works, the life they lived, and the example they set for us continue to inspire, encourage, and bless us when we recall them in our memory.

Self-Reflection: Moses, z"l—may his memory be a blessing. May I be inspired to finish stronger than I started. May I find the courage I see in Moses's life to lead—and leave—a legacy as a friend of God. May I fulfill all God has for me to do and be found faithful to the end. May my memory be a blessing one day.

Prayer: Father—thank You for how You love and guide me through Your Word. Thank You for the life of Moses! As an infant, he was hidden. In death, he was hidden. And in the middle, he lived a remarkable life as Your friend. I want to know what it means to be Your friend. Make my heart a place You can dwell. You are good. Your leadership in my life is perfect, and You can be trusted. Amen.

Daily Reading: Deuteronomy 32–34

REFERENCES

p. 86, Robert Emmons, Greater Good Essay: "Why Gratitude Is Good."

p. 101, Resting Place, Artist Brian Doerksen, Album Acoustic Worship: Isn't He, Released 1996